THE VALLEY BETWEEN

A MOTHER'S GUIDE TO FINDING PURPOSE AND PEACE AFTER PREGNANCY LOSS

THE VALLEY BETWEEN

A MOTHER'S GUIDE TO FINDING PURPOSE AND PEACE AFTER PREGNANCY LOSS

DR. JENNA ZIGLER

ethos collective

THE VALLEY BETWEEN © 2025 by Jenna Zigler. All rights reserved.

Printed in the United States of America

Published by Igniting Souls
PO Box 43, Powell, OH 43065
IgnitingSouls.com

This book contains material protected under international and federal copyright laws and treaties. Any unauthorized reprint or use of this material is prohibited. No part of this book may be reproduced or transmitted in any form or by any means, electronic or mechanical, including photocopying, recording, or by any information storage and retrieval system, without express written permission from the author.

LCCN: 2024927341
Paperback ISBN: 978-1-63680-444-6
Hardback ISBN: 978-1-63680-445-3
eBook ISBN: 978-1-63680-446-0

Available in paperback, hardcover, e-book, and audiobook.

All Scripture quotations, unless otherwise indicated, are taken from the Holy Bible, New International Version®, NIV®. Copyright © 1973, 1978, 1984, 2011 by Biblica, Inc.™ Used by permission of Zondervan. All rights reserved worldwide. www.zondervan.com The "NIV" and "New International Version" are trademarks registered in the United States Patent and Trademark Office by Biblica, Inc.™

Any Internet addresses (websites, blogs, etc.) and telephone numbers printed in this book are offered as a resource. They are not intended in any way to be or imply an endorsement by Igniting Souls, nor does Igniting Souls vouch for the content of these sites and numbers for the life of this book.

Some names and identifying details may have been changed to protect the privacy of individuals.

The superscript symbol IP listed throughout this book is known as the unique certification mark created and owned by Instant IP™. Its use signifies that the corresponding expression (words, phrases, chart, graph, etc.) has been protected by Instant IP™ via smart contract. Instant IP™ is designed with the patented smart contract solution (US Patent: 11,928,748), which creates an immutable time-stamped first layer and fast layer identifying the moment in time an idea is filed on the blockchain. This solution can be used in defending intellectual property protection. Infringing upon the respective intellectual property, i.e., IP, is subject to and punishable in a court of law.

For my boys—Jude, Bodhi, and Silas

Table of Contents

Foreword ix
Introduction xiii

Part I: The Depth of Grief 1

Chapter 1: Psalm 34:18 3
    Stepping Stones 8
Chapter 2: Matthew 5:4 9
    Stepping Stones 13
Chapter 3: Ecclesiastes 3:1-8 14
    Stepping Stones 20

Part II: Walking Through the Valley 21

Chapter 4: Psalm 23:4 23
    Stepping Stones 27
Chapter 5: 1 Peter 5:7 28
    Stepping Stones 33
Chapter 6: 2 Corinthians 1:3-4 35
    Stepping Stones 38

Part III: Light in the Valley ... 39

Chapter 7: Revelation 21:4 ... 41
    Stepping Stones ... 45
Chapter 8: Romans 8:18 ... 46
    Stepping Stones ... 50
Chapter 9: 1 Thessalonians 4:13 ... 51
    Stepping Stones ... 55

Part IV: God's Strength in the Valley ... 57

Chapter 10: Philippians 4:6-7 ... 59
    Stepping Stones ... 64
Chapter 11: Isaiah 41:10 ... 65
    Stepping Stones ... 69
Chapter 12: John 16:33 ... 70
    Stepping Stones ... 74

Part V: Finding Purpose in the Depths ... 75

Chapter 13: Romans 8:28 ... 77
    Stepping Stones ... 85
Chapter 14: Psalm 30:5 ... 86
    Stepping Stones ... 90
Chapter 15: 2 Corinthians 4:18 ... 91
    Stepping Stones ... 95

Conclusion ... 97
Acknowledgments ... 99
About the Author ... 101

Foreword

I have served as the founder and executive director of Sufficient Grace Ministries for Women, Inc for twenty-one years, walking with thousands of grieving mothers and families who have experienced pregnancy, infant, and child loss. Through the authoring of several books, resources, and presentations, I have told many of their stories, in addition to sharing my own journey through grief and loss.

God has faithfully woven beauty from the ashes of our grief as my husband and I walked through the loss of three of our five children in the early years of our marriage. I learned much about the true, nitty-gritty faith that comes when you are clinging to the hem of Jesus' garment in desperation, learning to believe Him when you do not see the answer to your prayers on this side of heaven. First, I lost my twin daughters, Faith and Grace, in 1996 at 26.5 weeks into my pregnancy and once more in 1998, when our son Thomas was diagnosed in the womb with a life-limiting condition known as Potter's Syndrome (absence of kidneys).

Thomas lived for six hours at his full-term birth. As I held him in my arms, rocked him, and sang to Him during his last moments on earth, I felt an indescribable peace and joy. I felt the presence of Jesus filling the room, reassuring me that He had not left or forsaken me or my son. It was the privilege of my life to be chosen as his mother, to be chosen to carry him, to be the voice he heard when he entered this world and the one singing to him as he was carried home to heaven by our Savior.

There were moments on that journey, waiting to meet our son, when I wondered if God's sufficient grace that He promises in 2 Corinthians 12:9 could possibly be enough for me to endure another labor that ended in another painful goodbye while standing beside a tiny grave. But His grace was indeed sufficient for me on that day, and I would walk those four and a half months of carrying Thomas, wandering in the faith wilderness, again and again to experience the time I had with him. I feel the same about my precious daughters, Faith and Grace, as well. I love and cherish my children in heaven fiercely, just as I do my living children.

I was honored when Jenna asked me to write the foreword for her book, *The Valley Between*. In reviewing this beautiful offering from her heart, I found that many of the same scriptures had resonated with my own journey through loss, pain, and grief. They are the ones I referred to in my pain and have referred others to as well. God's word is a healing balm for the agony that seems to have no answer or relief in the beginning. Those who find Him while standing on the sacred ground where heaven meets earth, a place I have often heralded as the closest we can be to feeling the full presence of Jesus this side of heaven, find the only peace and relief that can truly heal a wound so harsh and devastatingly deep as losing your child.

I have had the privilege of walking with thousands of mothers who are stumbling in, looking for a way to survive the pain. Those who muster the incredible courage to step toward God in the midst of the ugly raw agony of grief, to reach for His hand while they are in the pits of despair, to reach for Him even when they are angry and filled with bitterness that threatens to take root and taste only the bile of their pain and brokenness for a season—those are the ones who somehow not only endure the darkness of grief, but find their way back to the light. They find a way to more than survive but to allow God to weave their brokenness into a beautiful tapestry, growing their faith into something deeper and sweeter than they could ever have imagined before walking in the valley between who they were and who they would become.

Jenna is one of those courageous mothers, who kept stepping toward God in the pain, in the anger, in the grief, in the wandering. Sufficient Grace Ministries had the honor of walking with her when she met her sweet son, Bodhi. You will read more about Bodhi's diagnosis and their family's story as you walk through the pages of this book.

When Jenna wrote to me to tell me about her book project, she shared how SGM impacted her own journey. I was humbled and grateful that the words in my own books and the support that she felt from our community brought her comfort and peace. And, after reviewing her book, I am proud and blessed that she has reached a place in her healing to offer a voice of comfort and hope in the wilderness to another grieving heart on this path. Our God weaves beauty from ashes, and the lives of our children have great value and impact on others who walk this earth.

Our ministry mission is based on 2 Corinthians 1:3-4, which states *Praise be to the God and Father of our Lord Jesus Christ, the Father of compassion and the God of all comfort, who comforts us in all our troubles, so that we can comfort those in any trouble with the comfort we ourselves receive from God.*

Jenna is a precious embodiment of God's very words in this scripture. She stepped toward Him in her pain. She chose to lean into the Father of compassion, the God of all comfort. She allowed Him to comfort her in all of her troubles. And, through the miraculous grace of that comfort, she found her way through the wilderness to a new place where the missing and ache remain but also hope and possibility and a new path to a place where she could pour out the same comfort that God gave to her to the next mother on this journey. There are few things more precious on this earth than bearing witness to the gift of redeeming restoration. Only God can do that, and He chooses to weave that incredible tapestry of hope in the hearts of those who are willing to allow Him to heal them and to make them into willing vessels of His love.

The journey is messy, friend. It takes time and stumbling. You must walk through the pain, feel it, surrender to the tumultuous sea of grief for a time, and surrender to the only One who can carry you through it. It is not linear or tied up in a neat bow. But there is light on the other side to the one who endures. Keep stepping toward Him, dear one. And when you cannot take one more step, just rest and let Him come to you. One step at a time, one breath at a time. He holds your tears in a bottle and sits with you; even in the deepest pits—even when you cannot feel Him, He is there. He will never leave you, nor forsake you—no matter how bleak it feels. May you find solace in the pages of this book and in His word. Thank you, Jenna, for this beautiful offering of truth, comfort, and grace from another mother who has walked in the valley between.

—Kelly Gerken
Founder and Director of Sufficient Grace Ministries

Introduction

"I'm sorry. There is no heartbeat."

Our baby had died. Although we had just found out for sure, I had known it in my heart for at least thirty-six hours. We were on a medical mission trip in Jamaica when it happened. On a Sunday evening, I wasn't feeling up to socializing with the others on the trip, so I excused myself back to our room.

Just seven weeks earlier, we found out our baby boy had trisomy 18, a rare chromosomal disorder that meant our baby's life on Earth would likely be brief. At the advice of my midwife, I elected to continue with our mission trip and try to move on with my pregnancy in the most normal way possible.

Needless to say, my anxiety got the best of me that night, and I just needed a break from pregnancy congratulations and people touching my belly.

When I was safely back in our room, I started sobbing. Not the kind of cries you try to stifle in the presence of others but big, heaving cries. I pleaded with God to keep my baby safe. I cried out to Him, truly out loud, and asked for protection.

This wasn't the first time I had done this. Since learning of Bodhi's diagnosis, I spent plenty of time pouring my heart out to God. This wasn't anything new. I thought that if I prayed hard enough, maybe He would let me hold my baby alive. Maybe my son would be one of the miracle trisomy babies who would bless us with a few years here on Earth.

Shortly after I pleaded with God that night, I felt my little boy start leaping in my stomach. He was always way more active than our oldest son ever was, and this night, he was most definitely dancing in there. Or practicing his field goals.

I woke up the next morning—Monday morning—and we went to our eye clinic for the day. I didn't feel much movement that day, but I chalked it up to the heat and distractions of a hard work day seeing patients.

Then, Tuesday came. By midday, I knew he was gone. I hadn't felt him move since Sunday night that I could recall. I told my husband that night, and we decided to see a doctor first thing the next morning.

Finding a doctor to perform an ultrasound in Jamaica is a story of its own, but we finally arrived at a clinic that agreed to see me. I intently watched the screen as the doctor glided the ultrasound probe over my belly. No movement. No fluttering heart. No sound. As he removed the probe, I was already in tears.

His clinical, impersonal tone stung me to my core as I attempted to choke back tears and make it out of the room. The hot, cramped office seemed to evoke the opposite of what I felt—cold and alone.

As we left that day and flew home to deliver our son, I was honestly overwhelmed with anger. How could a loving God take this from me? How could a loving God allow this to happen? Why is this happening? Does He not care?

Introduction

Up until that moment in time, my life felt easy. I grew up in a good home with loving parents and siblings. We went to church every Sunday and said our prayers at night. I married an amazing man and already had a little boy who enriched my life like nothing I'd ever experienced. Our businesses were thriving. Life was good.

Until it wasn't.

In the months afterwards, I found myself curled up in a ball, crying uncontrollably at inopportune times. I dove into work to avoid having to think about the pain of this loss. I lost friends and isolated myself into a world full of grief and pain.

Shortly after we lost Bodhi, my grandfather died, and my dad was also diagnosed with Alzheimer's Disease at the young age of 60. My life suddenly felt like it was spiraling out of control. I was losing everyone and everything around me, and I suspect I'm not the only one who has ever felt this way.

This spiraling feeling doesn't have to be in response to terrible things like death and disease. We all have a plan in our heads about how life is supposed to look—how we want it to look. And when it happens to turn out the way we've hoped and prayed, we praise God for it. We remember to thank Him (hopefully) for the amazing work He's done in our lives.

But when it doesn't turn out our way? That's another story. When our expectations are not in line with reality, we begin to question His goodness. We may even question why we pray in the first place. Does God exist if He's not helping my life in any way? Does He really exist if I can't see or feel Him working?

Yet, it's important to remember that we are not the potter. We are not the creator of Earth and everything in it. God is.

In Jeremiah 18:6, the Lord says, "Can I not do with you, Israel, as this potter does?" declares the Lord. "Like clay in the hand of the potter, so are you in my hand, Israel." He already has a plan for you, for me, and for everyone else under heaven, and that plan will include pain and hardship whether we like it or not.

But that wasn't the original plan. God's original plan didn't include any pain, sin, or death. We live in a fallen world because of the decisions that Adam and Eve made long ago. When they made the decision to eat the forbidden fruit, it brought sin and death into this world. Because of this, we cannot avoid brokenness.

We know that as Christians, our lives will not be easy. In fact, God promises we will face tough times and trouble. John 16:33 states, "I have told you these things, so that in me you may have peace. In this world, you will have trouble. But take heart! I have overcome the world." I don't know about you, but that's a hard pill for me to swallow.

I'm sure that, just like me, you'd love to have an easy life without challenges. However, we know that won't be the case for anyone, and the most important part of all is how we deal with those challenges.

In the early days after losing Bodhi, I felt drawn to the Word like no other time in my life. Sure, I was angry at Him. I questioned Him. But I didn't know where else to turn, so I turned to God. I prayed hard for Him to take the pain away and for life to just return to normal.

I Googled grief verses and read through the book of Job for the first time. This book was recommended to me as a great place to start when dealing with grief. Job knew plenty of it!

I eventually read through the entire Bible quite a few times. I craved His love, and I eventually found it. But the road was never easy.

Introduction

I know the type of grief you're going through today in the loss of your child. It doesn't matter if it happened a few days ago or many years ago. You lost a piece of you. But I also know that we serve a loving God who is right by your side through it all. There is hope to be found in the grief you're feeling whether you have any idea who Jesus is or not.

Throughout these pages, I'm going to take you on a journey through scriptures that helped me navigate the depths and valleys of grief. We're going to talk about the really hard things, and you'll learn how to not be consumed by your grief.

We're then going to move toward hope and how you can find strength amidst the grief you're feeling. Grief is something that must be completely felt and processed, but there is so much hope and strength to be found in the process.

Finally, I can't wait to show you how to find purpose in your pain. I know you've been through a lot, but God would not have allowed it to happen without having a good, beautiful plan for your life. Remember, God has plans for your life that you cannot even comprehend.

If you're looking for a book to give you the physical details of loss and what to expect, this is not that book. This book is for your soul. It's for the very thing that makes you who you are. This book is for the lost soul who is grasping for understanding and a place to belong.

The valley of grief you're currently in lies between who you were before loss and who you become through it.[IP] It exists between the mountain of your past life and the mountain of your future healing, and it exists between devastating sorrow and eventual peace in this journey.

I can't wait to begin and see what's next for you.

PART I

The Depth of Grief

I sat alone in our dark living room, staring out at the bleak, gray sky. Was he up there watching over me? Was God up there with him? The house was so quiet it almost echoed. In the silence, I felt the weight of my grief settle around me like a heavy blanket, smothering my spirit.

The reality of losing my son hit me again with fresh intensity, and I was completely overwhelmed. I looked out the window at the cloudy Ohio sky, and it felt as if the world outside was mirroring what was happening in my heart. It was gray, heavy, and lifeless.

My husband and I had returned from a walk outside. It was our attempt to get out of the house and forget about the pain we were feeling. It's strange to say that now because it sounds like I wanted to forget about what happened.

However, that couldn't be further from the truth. It wasn't that I wanted to forget about our son or forget about the tragedy we'd just gone through. I just wanted to feel better. I wanted the pain to go away because I didn't know how to process it.

In the early days of grief, I had so many questions and so much anger. I felt more than alone. In the back of my mind, I wondered if God even cared. You might feel this way right now too. I want you to know that I see you. I feel your pain because I was there.

In this section, we're going to journey through the hardest parts of grief. We're going to discuss the early, dark days where nothing seems to be worth living for. And I'm hopefully going to lead you to find a bit of hope in the midst of it all.

1

Psalm 34:18

"The Lord is close to the brokenhearted and saves those who are crushed in spirit."

It's hard to describe how broken I felt in those early days, but "crushed" is the closest word I can find. I felt like my heart had shattered into pieces, and the weight of my grief was pressing down on every part of me—my mind, my soul, my body. I was crushed under the weight of loss, and if you've ever lost a child, you know exactly how this feels.

Let me pause here to let you know that it doesn't matter if you lost your baby before six weeks or full term or after they were born. There isn't a worst-case scenario here. They're all unimaginable, terrible losses that no one should ever have to experience. They're different experiences, yes, but every loss of a baby is the loss of a piece of you.

Your grief is valid. Your loss is valid, and please never let anyone tell you otherwise. We've all heard the platitudes people try to comfort us with. "It's for the best," or "It's God's will," or "Everything happens for a reason."

These not only minimize our grief but also imply it's not a big deal and we will "get over it" soon enough. Often, these sayings come from well-meaning people who honestly have no idea what to say when something like this happens.

So, while you may hear these phrases often in your early days of grief, I encourage you to process your grief as you see fit. Never let anyone tell you your grief isn't valid or your loss isn't significant. Losing someone you carried inside you and love with all your soul is absolutely crushing.

The word *crushed* means to press, squeeze, or bear down with such force that something is broken beyond repair. In those first few months, I was broken in a way that felt irreparable, as if my heart and spirit had been ground into dust.

At that moment, I couldn't imagine how I could ever be whole again. The pain was too great, and the loneliness of sitting in that quiet, empty house was almost unbearable. I didn't really have anyone close to me who had lost a baby. I felt so lost and so alone.

But Psalm 34:18 tells us, "The Lord is close to the brokenhearted and saves those who are crushed in spirit." What does this even mean? And what does it mean for Him to *save* those of us who are experiencing such pain?

When David wrote Psalm 34, he was in one of the darkest periods of his life. He was attempting to run from King Saul and escape and avoid capture by the Philistines. He even pretended to be insane in order to avoid being captured and killed.

These words from David were born from his lived experience. David knew what it felt like to be completely shattered and have his world crumbling around him. You may think of David as having a relatively easy life. He was anointed to be king of Israel, after all!

But at this moment, he found himself:

- Homeless
- Running for his life
- Separated from family and friends
- Living among enemies
- Having lost everything
- In constant danger

This sounds pretty intense to me, and I can't imagine what he could have been feeling, except a whole lot of loss and fear. This is similar to what you may be feeling right now.

But instead of being angry at God and cursing His name, he chose to praise God and convey to others how important it is to fear the Lord. When he asked God to help him, God helped him. David was feeling crushed (there's no question about that), but it was during those moments when he felt God move the most.

This psalm isn't just about suffering. It's about the intimate presence of God in our suffering. I know it's easy to feel isolated in grief. There were times when I thought no one could possibly understand the depth of my pain. But this verse reminds me that even though I'm physically alone at any given moment, I'm never spiritually alone.

He is close—closer than the silence, closer than the caving in walls of my house, closer than the heavy air I'm breathing. He isn't watching me from a distance; He is right there with me, in my brokenness.

I knew He wasn't going to take away the pain and the loss in an instant. But He did have the capability of lifting the weight from my shoulders, long enough to let me breathe for a bit.

Even in my anger towards God, He pulled me towards Him like nothing I can describe in the months directly after my loss. Every time I wanted to curse Him, every time I yelled out to Him with my anguish, I felt drawn to the Bible instead.

Looking back, I know this was Him working within me and through me. And He'll do the same for you. If you seek Him, He will sit next to you, hold you, and cry with you because He knows your innermost parts. He desires a relationship with you.

If you feel crushed today, you are not alone. You might be sitting in your own quiet, empty space, feeling the weight of your grief pressing down on you. But remember, many have gone before you. Here are just a few examples:

Job (Job 1: 13-22)

- Lost all ten children in one day
- Lost his wealth and health
- Grieved so deeply he tore his clothes and sat in ashes
- *Yet maintained his faith through intense suffering*

David (throughout 1 and 2 Samuel and Psalms)

- Lost his infant son from Bathsheba
- Lost his adult son Absalom
- Lost his best friend Jonathan
- All the other issues I mentioned above
- *Expressed raw grief (and praise) in many psalms*

Hannah (1 Samuel 1: 1-20)

- Experienced infertility and loss
- Was deeply grieved by her inability to have children
- *Poured out her grief to God at the temple*

Mary (Luke 2: 34-35 and John 19: 25-27)

- Witnessed her son Jesus's crucifixion
- Experienced the prophesied "sword piercing her soul"
- *Stood at the cross during His death*

All these Biblical examples have one thing in common. They went to God in their suffering. They poured out their grief to Him and maintained their faith in Him because He is the answer.

The Lord is close to you right now, even in this moment. He sees your broken heart, and He promises to save you. He's not going to remove the pain, but He can help you walk through this dark valley of grief without being smothered by it.

Life can break us in ways we never imagined. But the beauty of God's promise is that being crushed doesn't mean being forgotten. He is with you, right now, in the midst of your grief. And even though you may not feel it, He is already at work, healing the pieces of your heart and lifting some of the weight from your soul.

Stepping Stones

At the end of each chapter, I'm going to give you a little homework. Don't worry! These are simple things you can do to apply what you've learned from each highlighted verse and chapter. I'm calling these stepping stones because this implies careful, intentional progress. This is exactly what it takes to move through this difficult terrain of grief.

Talk to God

- If you haven't already, talk to God. Don't pay attention to your tone or even the words coming out of your mouth. Just start talking to Him whenever you need to get something off your chest. If you prefer to write your thoughts rather than speak them (I see you), find a journal or just a piece of paper and start writing until you can't write anymore.

- Find a Bible (if you don't already have one) or download the Bible app. Open it, and start reading. If you want to read about someone who knows grief, open to the book of Job. I think you'll be encouraged to see Job wrestle with his grief and relationship with God so intensely. He didn't blindly trust. He questioned. He was human, just like you and me.

2

Matthew 5:4

"Blessed are those who mourn,
for they will be comforted."

Up until this loss, I can't say I ever lost anything before. My great-grandmother had died while I was in high school. She entered heaven on September 11, 2001, of all dates. We used to joke that she saw everyone else going and had to hitch a ride. She was 96, and I had great, loving memories of her, but it wasn't a soul-crushing loss. She was ready to meet her Creator.

I had never lost anyone else close to me, to death anyway. I had moved across the country multiple times during my youth, from Michigan to Georgia and back again. Each time, I lost something—friends, mostly. It was hard to stay in touch when cell phones and Facebook didn't exist yet.

But those losses didn't touch the amount of grief and loss I was feeling either. I didn't have close friends who had lost babies, and no one in my family had, either. This was new territory for me, but thankfully, it was nothing new for God.

In Matthew 5:4, Jesus tells us, "Blessed are those who mourn, for they will be comforted."

If you're anything like me, all you're looking for is a little bit of comfort. On the hardest days, when I couldn't get out of bed and was in a deep, tough valley, I didn't need anyone to take away the pain. I just needed to feel comforted in the midst of it all. I needed to know that I was seen, heard, and validated in my grief.

You see, if you attempt to stuff away the pain and "move on" too quickly, it'll still rear its ugly head sooner or later. You can never get rid of grief completely, and it's necessary to move right on through it.

If you don't sit in these hard moments and let your body and mind succumb to the feelings you're experiencing—and truly experience them—you'll never be able to move forward. However, I'm not saying you have to do this alone.

Whenever I was having the worst time, God was there. I didn't always feel Him there, but because of Matthew 5:4, I know He's available to me because He promises comfort.

While you may not physically or even spiritually feel God near you in these moments, He can show up in unexpected ways. For me, He showed up through people. It came in ways I couldn't have predicted, from people I didn't expect. These moments felt like divine gifts of grace.

Women from my church group—women I was just getting to know—took time out of their busy schedules to visit, bring us dinner, and send us flowers and cards. I would answer the door in my sweats each time, falling into their arms as they told me how sorry they were for our loss.

While they didn't do anything profound, each small act of kindness was like a gentle whisper from God. We were seen. We were somehow being blessed in our mourning, and I felt the comfort.

These women were the hands and feet of Jesus in those early days, and I'll never be able to fully thank them for the impact they had on my family.

I'll also never forget the close friends who came and simply sat with us. They didn't try to fix our pain or say the perfect words to make us feel better—they just *sat* there. They let us cry, let us vent, let us grieve in whatever messy, raw way we needed to.

Sometimes, the most profound comfort comes not in words but in the silent companionship of those who are willing to sit in the darkness with you.[1P] Words can sometimes feel messy and inadequate in times like this, but silence and presence can be golden.

Those moments felt sacred, as if God Himself was sitting beside us, reminding us that it was okay to feel everything we were feeling.

And then there was our family. Our parents were with us in the hospital when we said our final goodbyes to our son. They wrote him letters, talked to him, and loved on him in that sacred space between Earth and heaven.

I'll never forget the strength and love they gave us in those moments. It was as if their presence was God's way of comforting us through the people who loved us most. We felt blessed that we didn't have to carry this grief alone.

Matthew 5:4 comes from Jesus' famous Sermon on the Mount. At this point in Jesus' ministry, the crowds following him were massive. I can only imagine the number of followers, disciples, and other onlookers He drew in way before the internet was a thing.

The Sermon on the Mount was Jesus' most comprehensive teaching on how to live a Godly life. This specific verse comes right at the beginning and is part of the Beatitudes. The Beatitudes were a series of statements describing the ideal follower of Jesus and their rewards, both present and in the future.

When Jesus talks about mourning, He's talking about a soul-crushing mourning just like you and I have experienced. And since He knows what's coming, He knows He'll also experience this same grief over his friend Lazarus and His own death on the cross.

I love that this verse is written to apply to us even now. He validates our grief while promising that in our deepest sorrow, we will experience God's deepest love and comfort. As we discussed in the last chapter, David felt God's presence the most when he was struggling. It's often the same for you and me!

Looking back, these visits from friends and family are a few of the ways God showed up for me in my grief. We're never directly blessed by the pain itself but by the way God meets us right there in its depths.

It's easy to feel isolated, to believe that no one could possibly understand the depth of your pain.

But God's promise in Matthew 5:4 is that we *will* be comforted.

You may not feel that way right away, but He is working in your life for good. He is using the people around you to carry some of the burden and to remind you that you're seen and loved. The blessing may not be in our timing or exactly how we think it will be, but it *will* come. He promises that it will.

Stepping Stones

Write Down Gratitudes

- Take some time to write down five things you're grateful for. This is a great way to realize the many blessings that you have in your life, even amidst soul-crushing grief. Don't forget about the little things, either, because those are often more meaningful than the big things.

- Make gratitude a daily habit. Whether you do this first thing in the morning or right before bed, keep a record of what you're grateful for. I promise this simple practice will change your life.

3

Ecclesiastes 3:1-8

"There is a time for everything, and a season for every activity under the heavens: a time to be born and a time to die, a time to plant and a time to uproot, a time to kill and a time to heal, a time to tear down and a time to build, a time to weep and a time to laugh, a time to mourn and a time to dance, a time to scatter stones and a time to gather them, a time to embrace and a time to refrain from embracing, a time to search and a time to give up, a time to keep and a time to throw away, a time to tear and a time to mend, a time to be silent and a time to speak, a time to love and a time to hate, a time for war and a time for peace."

I came across this verse a year or so after our loss, when the fog finally felt like it was lifting from our lives. As I dug into what it was saying, I realized our lives are indeed made up of seasons. Some call them spring, summer, fall, and winter, like Richard Blackaby in The Seasons of God.[1] Another way to describe them is through this verse.

The year we lost Bodhi was devastating for our family—emotionally, mentally, and financially. We lost multiple loved ones in a short period. We lost our entire life savings (a story for a different book). We saw our world attempt to navigate an unprecedented global pandemic. We watched our business flounder.

Two months after losing our son, my grandfather died from heart issues he had been battling for only a few months. I went to visit him shortly after our loss, and he was so sweet, telling me he was sorry to hear about the loss of our baby.

He and my grandmother had lost two babies years ago, and I can't imagine the pain they went through. There's now no shortage of bereavement groups and hospital support staff well-versed in baby loss. But at that time, they really had few people to lean on but each other.

That year was our time to uproot, tear down, weep, mourn, give up, and hate (although I dislike that word). But as we made our way out of that year—that winter—spring began to show its face.

We slowly started to build our business and life savings back up. I started diving into the Word on a daily basis, and we made it a point to be active participants in our church.

Thankfully, the seasons of our lives change, and we get to come out of winter eventually. With time, I've come to trust that even in the hardest seasons, when we don't feel Him or see Him working, God is at work. This didn't happen overnight, and it's ok to continue to wrestle with it. I still do.

---

[1] Richard Blackaby, *The Seasons of God: How the Shifting Patterns of Your Life Reveal His Purposes for You*. PRH Christian Publishing, 2012.

While we all would love to dictate the seasons our life endures, we have to remember that, again, we are not the potter. God created you and me for a specific purpose, with specific experiences to shape us into who He wants us to become. No matter how much we fight it, the seasons will change and, at least in my life, they seem to change in exactly the correct order.

When you're in the true depths of grief and the early stages of this nightmare, remember that grief is a natural part of the human experience. This is a winter season, and it's meant to happen like any other season.

Sometimes, winters are long and unforgiving. They strip us to the core and begin to reveal who we really are by the time it starts to warm up again. The same is true with grief.

Winter is often when we'll struggle with God the most. Because of this, I started a community called the Miscarriage and Pregnancy Loss Support Group on Facebook. This Christian community brings together mothers who have lost a child, and it's been an amazing resource for so many when they have nowhere else to turn.

I asked my community how their relationship with God had been affected by their loss. Were they closer to Him, or did they feel further away? I received so many insightful responses from women deep in the valley of grief. Here are a few:

> *"I was always raised that God was good and merciful…but I won't lie, my faith has been shaken. I don't understand; I'm hurting. I know I don't know all, maybe it was a merciful thing because I don't know what the future could have held. But I am still shaken."* —Esther

> *"I am angry at God right now, but I have never leaned on him more than I have now. It has been my comfort to know*

my sweet boy is up there with him. I know my anger won't last forever, but I have found so much comfort in Him." —Chelsea

"I was so angry with God when this happened. I prayed and begged him every single day to bless us with our boy. When I saw no heartbeat on the ultrasound, I felt like I was being punished. I have apologized for being so angry with him, but it's been really, really hard to understand." —Ashley

"Both. At first it kind of had me angry and disappointed with God but as the years have gone by, I remind myself that if it is ordained by God, then it will be. My husband and I have had seven losses with no living biological children yet, but my relationship with God is as strong as ever now." —Ashley

"It has made me distant. I have tried a few times to go back to church, but I'm just so angry and full of questions. I don't and can't understand why. I had two miscarriages, finally made it past the high-risk stage, and the cord got around my daughter's neck. Why? The miscarriages weren't hard enough? Then, without trying, I got pregnant and lost that baby to miscarriage. I'm just so angry and full of rage over it all." —Tonia

"I was surprised, kind of. But it brought me so much closer to the Lord. The peace I have now truly surpasses all understanding." —Mariah

As you can see from the responses I received, everyone feels this pain differently. This winter season brings a lot of hurt, anger, guilt, and questioning. If you're feeling discouraged today, know that you are not alone.

Just as there is a time to laugh, there is also a time to weep. It's important to acknowledge that grieving is part of the rhythm of life, just as the happier seasons are.

You might not want to hear this right now, but I find it comforting to know that even Jesus grieved. John 11:35 says "Jesus wept" after he heard that his friend Lazarus had died.

Now, this has always struck me as interesting because Jesus also knew that He would be raising Lazarus from the dead. He knew that He would soon be rejoicing with everyone else, yet He took time to grieve.

Another example is when Jesus wept over the circumstances surrounding Jerusalem (very near to his own death). Luke 19:41 says, "As he approached Jerusalem and saw the city, he wept over it."

This was supposed to be a triumphant entrance into the city, a time for rejoicing. However, Jesus knew what was about to happen, who would betray Him, and the people who would be hurt in the process.

His tears in both of these examples remind us that He knows what we're going through and He truly cares for you and me. He's not expecting you to suppress your feelings. He's expecting you to do the exact same thing He did: grieve, cry, and be alone.

So why does God allow seasons—even the deep valleys of grief and death? He allows them because He is constantly molding us, shaping us into who He has destined us to become.

He often uses hardship to bring us closer to Him and into a deeper relationship with Him so we're able to fulfill His ultimate plan for our lives. He wants us to become more like Him. This is called sanctification, and hardship is often a stepping stone in accomplishing this.

Ecclesiastes 3:1-8

God allows us to walk through seasons, not as a punishment or an arbitrary cycle, but as part of His divine plan. Each season, no matter how painful, serves a purpose in shaping us, in molding us into who we are meant to become.[IP]

In the depths of grief, it can feel as though the cold will never break and the darkness will never lift. But the very nature of seasons is that they *change*. No season lasts forever. Spring comes. The sun breaks through the clouds, and life begins to bloom again, even after the harshest winter. That's the promise I cling to, and it's a promise for you, too.

Ecclesiastes 3:1-8 reminds us that it's okay to feel the full range of human emotions, just like Jesus did. When the verse says there is "a time for everything," it's suggesting that God sovereignly oversees all of life's seasons, both joyful and painful.

There is a time for everything—a time to weep and a time to laugh; a time to mourn and a time to dance. These words reassure me that God sees every tear we shed, and He also knows the joy that is to come, even if we can't see it yet.

As you navigate your own season of grief, I encourage you to lean into God's timing. Trust that the One who created the seasons has a plan for this season of your life too. Remember that it's easy to see God's hand in seasons of joy, but He's just as present in seasons of sorrow. If you seek him during *all* seasons, healing will occur. These verses acknowledge the fullness of our human experience.

While you may not understand why Winter is here, you can trust that Spring will follow. In His perfect timing, healing will come. And in the meantime, remember that even in the darkest moments, you are not walking through this valley alone. God is with you, guiding you, comforting you, and preparing your heart for the new life yet to come.

Stepping Stones

Document Your Seasons

- Think back on your life and identify times when you felt you were in Winter, Spring, Summer, and Autumn. Notice how your life has shifted through these seasons, never staying in one season for very long. Use the following descriptions, based on The Seasons of God, to guide you:
    - **Winter.** This is a season of endings and closure. It can also be a season of rest or reflection.
    - **Spring.** This season is about possibility and potential. It's a time of new beginnings and the excitement that comes with them.
    - **Summer.** This season is about growth. It follows something that started in the Spring and is now maturing.
    - **Autumn.** This is the apex of a season in life. It's the graduation, the promotion, or the big break.

PART II

Walking Through the Valley

Grief is not something we leave behind in an instant, nor is it something we can conquer in a day. This journey is a long, winding walk through a valley where darkness often looms overhead.

And grief is like the hiking pack you always have with you, bringing it along because it's necessary.[IP] You can't get rid of it, or you wouldn't have everything you need. You'd love to toss it aside, leave it somewhere on the trail, or even heave it down a mountain. But grief doesn't work like that.

This valley and your little hiking pack are a reality for anyone who has experienced profound loss like this. There are moments when the pain feels like too much to bear, the valley seems endless, and the pack seems unbearably heavy. There are times when God's presence feels distant, even though we know He's with us.

In this part of the book, I want to walk with you through that valley. We're going to take grief along for the ride because, if we're honest, we can't get rid of it anyway. Together, we will explore the evolution of grief, how it changes over time, and how God remains our constant in the midst of our deepest pain if we let Him be so.

4

Psalm 23:4

*"Even though I walk through the darkest valley,
I will fear no evil, for you are with me; your rod
and your staff, they comfort me."*

The hospital room was eerily quiet that night, but my heart was anything but. It felt like I was trapped in a nightmare I couldn't wake up from. I had just been induced to eventually deliver our son. I'd sent my husband home to get some sleep (so at least one of us could).

I fell in and out of sleep that night, but if I'm honest, I'm not sure I slept at all. I had incredibly intense cramping all night, pain much worse than my first natural childbirth. I remember thinking what a cruel joke it was that women have to endure this type of pain to deliver a child they will never get to take home.

I called my husband back to the hospital early in the morning. I knew our son was coming, and although I thought I was ready, I had no idea what was in store for me.

Before his diagnosis, I had never realized I would have to actually give birth to him. I'm not sure what I thought would happen, but I didn't even know I had to endure labor to meet him, just like I would if he were alive. Maybe this is you, too. I was blissfully naive.

I often think about this naivete and wish I could have it back. But I know God doesn't desire for us to stay naive forever. He pushes us to grow and change and become more Christ-like, and it often involves a lot of heartache to get there.

After my son's diagnosis, I read a book about carrying a child whose life was expected to be brief. A Gift of Time by Amy Kuebelbeck and Deborah L. Davis, Ph.D.[2] didn't shy away from the details, and I will forever be grateful for that. But here I was, still expecting that I'd be spared some of the pain.

He was born that morning after ten hours of labor, and I was in awe of him. He looked so perfect and peaceful, and so much like his older brother. I remember looking at his tiny face and at his little body, trying to memorize every detail. I knew that these final moments were all we had left.

We spent the entire day getting pictures with him, holding him, and whispering our love to him. We were trying to parent him in whatever way we could—because this was it. This was the last time we would ever see him, the last time we would ever hold him.

The world outside felt like it was moving on, but for us, time had stopped. There was an oppressive heaviness in the air, and we were literally in the valley of the shadow of death, as some versions of the Bible state. This was our last day with our son. We knew it, and it broke us.

---

[2] Amy Kuebelbeck and Deborah L. Davis, PhD. *A Gift of Time: Continuing Your Pregnancy When Your Baby's Life is Expected to be Brief.* Johns Hopkins University Press, 2011.

After spending all day with him, well after we had sent our parents and oldest son home to bed, my husband and I looked at each other, and we both knew it was time to let him go. When the nurse finally came to take him away, my heart shattered in a way I didn't think was possible. I cried harder than I've ever cried in my life.

This nurse was a woman we barely knew. She had entered our lives for only a fleeting few hours, but she was about to do something that would forever alter the course of our lives. She was going to take our son away, and we would never see him again.

As I watched her wheel him out through the door in his little cot, it felt like my soul was leaving with him. Where were we supposed to go from here? How were we supposed to continue living after this?

We packed up our things and drove home in silence that night. I didn't have anything to say, and I definitely didn't know what I was feeling enough to express it to anyone. I felt so numb.

I'll say it again because I'm sure you've felt it too. At that moment, I was so sad and angry. Angry with God. Angry that He would allow this to happen. Angry that my son was gone, and I had nothing to show for the labor my body had been through except a stuffed teddy bear given to me by the remembrance photographer. All I could think about was my son and myself.

For weeks, I felt selfish. I'm sure I didn't check in with my husband like I should have. I'm also sure I was distant with our two-year-old. He got to meet his brother, and I know he was somewhat aware of what was happening. I just didn't know how to process what I was feeling.

Looking back, I'm incredibly grateful for the comfort team that came into our room that day. I'm thankful for the photos and the mementos they helped us create because I know not everyone gets that kind of support. And I'm even thankful for the comfort bear they gave to me, so that my arms wouldn't feel so empty walking out of the hospital.

Sometime later, I came across Psalm 23:4, which says, "Even though I walk through the darkest valley, I will fear no evil, for you are with me; your rod and your staff, they comfort me."

I didn't feel comforted while at the hospital or on the way home. I felt broken. I felt lost. As I sat on that uncomfortable hospital bed, watching the nurse wheel my son away, I just didn't feel comforted by God yet. It seemed to be just me and my husband, attempting to comfort each other through a pain we'd never experienced before.

This psalm that David wrote draws deeply from his early experiences tending sheep in the Judean wilderness. The background is crucial because David isn't writing from theoretical knowledge. He intimately understood both the shepherd's heart and the sheep's complete dependence on their shepherd.

The phrase "valley of the shadow of death" refers to a deep, dark ravine like what he may have encountered. In Israel's landscape, shepherds often had to lead their flocks through dangerous valleys to reach better pastures. These valleys were often narrow, dark, and filled with potential dangers from predators or flash floods.

It makes for a great analogy in our discussion of the valley of our darkest grief. David isn't saying God promises we'll be free of the valleys or that He'll free us from them. But he is saying we'll have God's complete companionship and comfort through them.

As I walked through my own deep, dark valley in the months after our loss, I felt little nudges to open my Bible, to read what was there. I now know He was always present in my valley of grief, even when I was too blinded by my own pain to notice.

If you're feeling pain and anger today, He sees you. If you're feeling like your loss is somehow your fault, know that it's not. If you're feeling guilty for letting your baby or your partner down, know that this is a very normal feeling to have right now. All of this brokenness is normal and valid for a loss like this.

So if you're in that valley right now, I want you to know that you don't have to walk this path alone. God is with you. He sees your pain, He knows your anger, and He's not afraid of it. I promise. He'll continue to walk with you throughout your life, even carrying your hiking pack if you let Him.

Stepping Stones

Remember the Details

- Take time to write down every single detail you remember about your baby and your experience, no matter how brief their life. This could include everything from finding out you were pregnant to delivering your baby and saying goodbye. Think about all the details, both physical and emotional. Include how you felt about God, and, if you have a partner, include how you felt about them. This is particularly important to do if you have no other keepsakes from your baby, such as photographs. Whether you believe it or not, these memories are worth preserving. Note that this process can be very painful, but this will help you fully process the grief you're experiencing.

5

1 Peter 5:7

"Cast all your anxiety on Him because He cares for you."

I'm an anxious person by nature. I'm constantly thinking about what's next, and I often find myself stressed about things that haven't even happened yet. They've only happened in my mind, of course.

Needless to say, grief only made this worse. I worried about whether or not I would ever feel better. I worried about my husband and how he was handling the situation. I worried about losing our oldest son to some freak accident. I worried about our business, our future, and what would happen if we ever tried to get pregnant again.

It was utterly exhausting.

In the months after, while still very much in the valley of grief, we picked up and moved our lives across the country.

This was far from family, far from home, and far away from the hospital where we said goodbye. We needed a new start.

But actually, we had it all perfectly planned from the beginning (so we thought). We had been tossing around the idea of moving across the country when we had our twenty-week ultrasound and found out our son had a "lethal diagnosis." Unfortunately, those were the doctor's exact words.

We knew if he survived the pregnancy and birth, we would need extra support. So we delayed our move and decided to stay put.

After losing him, it felt like the perfect time for us to get away. I know God had his hands all over this plan from the start; we just didn't know what His timing would be. And that's often the toughest part.

God calls us to surrender, to let go of our plans and submit to His. In those broken moments, when we questioned whether or not we should still leave, He nudged us to go. We weren't running away from the problem but rather following the next stepping stone God had laid out for us.

The act of casting our anxieties onto God requires trust that He will carry the burden when we feel too weak. He is always in control.

I'm never going to say that moving away was easy. We left behind friends and family who were very important to us, but we knew we had to find out where this move would lead.

This chapter's highlighted verse is from a letter Peter wrote to Christians facing persecution and suffering. These believers were experiencing social ostracism, legal discrimination, and even physical threats because of their faith.

Many had lost homes, businesses, and relationships. They had great anxiety about their future, their safety, and their families. In this verse, he's encouraging others to rely on God, casting (or throwing) their cares on Him.

But I'll be honest. This is so hard to do. God calls us to cast our cares and anxieties on Him, meaning He will deal with them. He will take all of the burden from us. However, this is not how my brain inherently works, so I struggle with this.

Since I was little, I've always wanted to do the right thing, say the right thing, and make things right. I've always followed the rules and, therefore, also experience anxiety when things don't go as I thought they would.

Yet God is always available, asking us to cast our cares on Him. He already knows every difficult situation and anxiety we struggle with. He's already overcome it all, so what I need to do is *trust* that He means what He says.

When we experience the deep pain of losing a baby, our ability to trust God often feels shaken to its core. This kind of loss uniquely challenges our faith. It involves not just the loss of our precious child but also the loss of all our plans for the future.

The anxiety that follows frequently stems from a newfound fear of trusting God again. After all, if this could happen once, what's to prevent it from happening again? And there are many women out there who have lost babies again and again without answers as to why.

Trust becomes particularly difficult for several key reasons:

- **Past Pain**

    Our experience of loss fundamentally changes how we view safety and security in the world. Previous experiences of loss, whether related or unrelated to pregnancy, create layers of fear that can feel impossible to move past. As humans, we naturally seek control as a way to protect ourselves from further pain.

- **Uncertainty**

    We can't see God's plan, and this limitation often feels more acute after loss. We struggle to understand why bad things happen, especially to innocent babies. The future now feels threatening and uncertain.

- **Fear**

    The fear of experiencing another loss can be paralyzing. We become afraid of hurting again, of opening our hearts to hope only to have them broken. This fear often manifests as a reluctance to surrender control, even when we know control is an illusion.

But there are practical ways we can begin rebuilding our trust in God. Here are a few that have worked for me:

- **Take Small Steps**

    Begin with tiny moments of surrender, like letting go of anxiety for just one minute at a time. Talk to God, and tell him exactly what burden you'd like Him to take from you. Practice trust in less threatening situations before tackling bigger fears. Think of trust as a muscle that needs gradual strengthening. You wouldn't start with the heaviest weights at the gym, and you don't need to start with your biggest fears here.

- **Remember God's Faithfulness**

    Take time to look back at the evidence of God's care in your life, even in the midst of loss. We've discussed a bit about gratitude journaling already. Consider keeping a journal of answered prayers and things that have gone well in your life. These can be very small things. Practice noticing the small blessings that show God's presence in your daily life. Remember, He is there even when you can't feel or see Him working.

- **Study God's Character**

    This may be the toughest one if you've never opened a Bible before, but I encourage you to start learning about who God is. If the Bible intimidates you, open the Bible app and find a devotional on God's character or grief. Start to find peace in knowing that while our experiences may change, God's character remains consistent.

I want to also emphasize the second half of the verse—*because He cares for you*. Grief can make us feel isolated or forgotten, but this verse is a reminder that God deeply cares for us, especially in our suffering.

After we made our move across the country, we quickly joined a church and a new life group that poured into us each week. We knew we needed the support, and I felt an immediate call to open up about our current struggles. To put it plainly, our life there would not have been the same without this group of people.

When the pandemic hit not even one month later, they cared for our son when his daycare shut down. They gave us the space we needed to rebuild our business and process our grief. I know God cares for you and me, and I know he placed them in our lives for this exact reason.

But what do you do if you don't have anyone around you for support? God asks us to cast our anxieties on HIM. You don't need anyone else around you to do this. I've already given you a few tips to get started. This could look like jumping into the Word and reading your Bible every morning or evening. It could look like journaling prayers, meditating on scripture, or simply crying out to Him in your darkest moments. Then, quiet yourself and wait for Him to speak.

That last part has always been hard for me because, as you know by now, I'm anxious. I like to figure out the plan, finalize the plan, follow the plan. Plans help me avoid anxiety, right?

But when we're constantly planning our lives to the very second, leaving no space for God to interject and speak to us, we're never going to see the full glory of God's plan for us. We have to be quiet. We have to stop talking. We have to stop planning, even just for a few minutes.

When you do this, you'll find that God will start to speak to you. Hint: it's never with a scream, sometimes with a whisper, and usually with a nudge or feeling. And there's so much freedom in that.

When you finally feel God moving in your life, you'll realize you don't have to carry the weight of grief and anxiety alone. God invites us to trust Him with our pain, and in doing so, we can find the peace we've been yearning for.

Stepping Stones

Practice Surrender

- This chapter was all about trust and surrender, so that's what I'm going to recommend you practice. After losing a baby, when trust feels especially difficult, this small practice can help build your faith muscles. The next time anxiety strikes, try this practice: Set a timer for sixty seconds. Consciously give your worry to God for just that minute. Or ignore the timer and just go for it. This helps train your heart to turn to God as your first response to anxiety. Tell Him what you're worried about, tell Him you're giving it to Him, and then be silent. As this becomes easier and you begin to recognize anxiety creeping in, you can gradually increase the time during which you talk and listen to Him.

6

2 Corinthians 1:3-4

"Praise be to the God and Father of our Lord Jesus Christ, the Father of compassion and the God of all comfort, who comforts us in all our troubles, so that we can comfort those in any trouble with the comfort we ourselves receive from God."

I nervously walked into the brightly lit room, which seemed much too bright for a place where I'd be sharing my deepest grief with others. A part of me craved a dimly lit room, a space to hide in the shadows away from my feelings. But there I was anyway.

As I sat down in the circle, I looked around and noticed that I wasn't the only one who had walked in with their head down, avoiding eye contact. We were all broken. We were all anxious to see what this would bring.

An in-person therapy group was recommended to me after our loss, and I jumped right in. That's usually how I do things. I knew I needed someone to talk to, someone who might understand. We lost our son on Saturday, and by the next Thursday, I was sitting in a room of strangers who had also recently lost babies or children.

Many were surprised I was there already, but deep down, I knew I needed to be there. As our discussion progressed, I heard everyone's story—some incredibly tragic (although it's all tragic, isn't it?). And over the next few weeks, I came to know these people as members of the same club we never asked to be a part of.

Although we may feel broken in our grief, God can use that brokenness to bring healing to others. This new "club" was transformative in helping me feel less alone. It also helped me see how I could help others with their pain.

Over time, I began to realize I wasn't just there for me. My presence in the group wasn't just about receiving comfort. It was also about offering it. Because God had begun to give me glimpses of comfort in my grief, I was then able to relay that comfort to others.

One particular relationship became incredibly important. I clicked instantly with a woman who had lost two babies. One of her children had Down syndrome, a similar diagnosis to my son's.

As my first night at the support group was winding down and people were saying their goodbyes, she beelined right for me. "I feel so drawn to you," she said. "I'm so sorry to hear about your son. You're so brave for being here already."

She gave me a big hug, and I couldn't help but think about how she had lost not one but two babies. She didn't have any living children or a husband for support. But our differences didn't matter. We clicked right away because our losses were so similar. We had a good idea of what the other had been through.

2 Corinthians 1:3-4

Even after I moved away, we continued to stay in contact for years, being resources for each other. We would send texts back and forth, praying for each other, wishing happy birthday to our babies, or just checking in. This was exactly what I needed then, and it gave me so much comfort. I hope I was a comfort for her as well.

God gently led me to see that my grief had a purpose beyond my own healing. Maybe I was meant to be a source of comfort for others, just as He had been comforting to me.

This valley of grief is long, hard, and often feels isolating. But I believe that God wants to use your story to point others to His comfort.

In 2 Corinthians 1: 3-4, we hear from Paul, who had recently faced intense personal suffering. Near-death experiences, persecution, and deep emotional pain from conflicts within the church are things Paul knew well. So when he speaks about comfort in our pain, we can be sure he knows what he's talking about.

Comfort, in this case, doesn't just mean sympathy but more of a coming alongside. Paul goes on to say that because of God's love and comfort, there can be an overflow onto others around us who may need comforting in their time of need.

The great thing about it is that you don't have to join an in-person therapy group to show His love and comfort to others. When you begin to open up about your grief and your struggles, you invite others into the valley with you.[IP]

While it seems like an incredibly uncomfortable place to be, this is where true healing can occur. You may have a friend struggling with her own trouble, and it may not even be about grief. But you can still be a light for her and show her how God has comforted you in your deepest pain.

While grief can feel unbearable, God promises to use it for good. The comfort you'll receive from Him will not only bring you healing, but it will equip you to be a source of comfort for others.

Many of you are still in the depths of this dark grief valley, unsure of how you'll ever crawl your way out and find peace again. But just as God comforted me, He is there to comfort you, too. We'll discuss this even more in the coming chapters, but God will use your story in a way you can't even imagine. Remember that His plan is always good. He's always a source of comfort for you, and you can be a light in someone else's valley[IP].

Stepping Stones

Share Your Story

- If you haven't already, look for an online support group.[3] There are so many free resources out there, and I encourage you to find one that fits you. Then, share your story with the group. While it may be difficult to get your story out, it is incredibly cathartic to do so. You'll likely notice how others in the group come alongside you, and you will feel truly seen in your grief. Remember, there are so many others who have experienced similar losses and are waiting to hear about yours so they can feel less alone.

---

[3] https://www.facebook.com/groups/pregnancylossgroup

PART III

Light in the Valley

I read many, many books about heaven in the months after losing Bodhi. I would put in my headphones, turn on my audiobook, and run a few miles. I'm not sure I ever made it through one run without having to stop, dry my tears, and catch my breath.

I was so interested in heaven because I knew the only way to see him again was there. And while those books were inspired by everyone from children to neurosurgeons, they each gave me a sense of the same thing—hope.

As I listened to the different near-death experiences, I tried to imagine what it would be like. Many people describe seeing someone they know right away, almost welcoming their souls into this sacred place. Surely, Bodhi would be there. My grandfathers, too. And one day, all who have surrendered their lives to Him.

I finally began to see beyond the veil of grief that had shrouded me for so long. Yes, the pain was still there—a dull ache that I knew would never fully disappear. But alongside it, something new was growing. Hope in the promise of reunion. Hope in the assurance that death doesn't have the final say.

You know by now that grief is a long, winding valley without a clear destination. We keep moving forward, and time keeps moving on with grief by our sides. But as I've walked this path, I've come to realize it's not a journey that leads to nowhere. Instead, it's a journey that, when walked with faith, leads us to a deeper understanding of God's love and the hope of eternity.

In this section, we're going to explore that hope. We're going to look at how, even in our deepest grief, God offers us the promise of redemption. This redemption will never erase the pain you are feeling right now, but it will transform it and infuse it with a little hope.

As we continue on, I want you to know that it's okay if hope feels distant right now. It's ok if you're still angry at God or unsure of what this even means. Grief has its own timeline, and there's no rushing through it.

But I also want you to know that hope is there for you to find. It's found in the promises of God, in the love of those around us, and in the eternal life that awaits us.

7

Revelation 21:4

"He will wipe every tear from their eyes. There will be no more death or mourning or crying or pain…"

There's a song that gets me every time: "One Day" by Cochren & Co.[4] Maybe you know it.

One day, there'll be no more lives taken too soon.
One day, there'll be no more need for a hospital room.
One day, every tear that falls will be wiped by His hand…
We will see the promised land.

Each time this song comes on the radio or plays at church, I'm a complete mess. Tears stream down my face relentlessly, but I know it's because I feel God closer than ever in those

---

[4] www.cochrenmusic.com/one-day

moments. And because I know that Bodhi is with God, I feel him closely in those moments too.

Can you imagine a place where there will be no more death, mourning, crying, or pain? Can you imagine not having to wipe painful tears from your eyes because you're standing right there, staring into the faces of your loved ones and the face of God? It seems too good to be true sometimes, but this is exactly what God promises.

I imagine that this place we call heaven appears different for everyone in our own minds. Maybe for you, it's vivid color and sunshine. Maybe it's the feeling of being fully complete or the feeling of everlasting, unconditional love.

Whether it's right to do or not, imagining my little piece of heaven is something I've come to use as a coping mechanism. The scientific term for this coping strategy is compartmentalization. According to *Psychology Today*, compartmentalization is a defense mechanism where you mentally separate emotions, thoughts, or experiences to avoid discomfort.[5]

I didn't realize I was doing it until I had a recent discussion with my Christian counselor. I now realize that I use a specific mental box any time intense feelings of grief arise.

So, anytime I feel overwhelmed by grief or flooded with emotions around our loss, I imagine my little family in this "box" of a bright, sunny field. It's surrounded by tall pine trees on four sides and blue sky above. The field is always sunny and warm. My boys are running around my husband and me, enjoying a beautiful afternoon.

In the early months after losing him, I would imagine Bodhi in a little basket in the middle of the field, hanging out

---

[5] "Compartmentalization." *Psychology Today*, 2025. www.psychology-today.com/us/basics/compartmentalization. Accessed 5 March 2025.

with us. But my mind no longer goes there. He's no longer on the ground with us, but he's now in Jesus's arms looking down on us with love.

When used intentionally, this coping mechanism has helped me deal with my grief in the hardest moments. It's also helped me to imagine what heaven will be like. God promises that He will wipe every tear from our eyes. Will we remember the pain we felt on Earth? I'm not sure, but I can imagine we likely won't worry too much about it anymore since our souls will be healed in heaven.

Revelation was written by John, one of Jesus' closest disciples. He wrote this book while in exile, meaning he was forced to leave his country. The early Christians were also facing intense persecution, which wasn't anything new. But this book offered hope by revealing God's ultimate victory and the restoration of all things. This chapter specifically describes the new heaven and new Earth. It expresses the final state of perfect restoration for our souls and our world.

What makes John's perspective particularly interesting is that he had personally experienced deep grief. He had:

- Witnessed Jesus's crucifixion firsthand
- Been given responsibility for caring for Mary, Jesus's mother
- Seen many fellow apostles martyred
- Experienced persecution and exile himself
- Watched the early church suffer intense persecution

Yet, despite all this suffering, John's writings (including Revelation) are filled with hope. They're filled with the assurance of God's ultimate victory.

When he writes about God wiping away every tear in Revelation 21:4, he's writing as someone who had shed many tears himself. This gives me hope, judging by the number of tears I've shed in my life.

This verse doesn't only speak of an end to tears; it promises an end to death, mourning, crying, and pain. It's a complete restoration, a return to the world as it was meant to be in the beginning. As God intended it to be.

When thinking of Bodhi, of both of my grandfathers, of all those we've lost, I no longer just see the pain of separation. I see a future reunion in a place where pain and loss are merely distant memories.

Does this mean we should try to stop grieving now? Absolutely not. Our tears are sacred to God, and He understands our pain. Remember, Jesus cried and felt pain just as we do on this Earth.

But this promise gives us permission to grieve with hope. It allows us to look forward to a day when our pain will be transformed into joy. We can look forward to when our losses will be restored, and we'll understand the full picture of God's love and plan for us.

If you're in a place today where hope seems distant and pain feels all-consuming, I encourage you to hold onto this promise. Let it be an anchor for your soul. Our tears are not wasted—they're seen, known, and one day will be tenderly wiped away by our Creator. Until that day comes, we can find comfort in knowing that every tear brings us closer to the day we'll see our babies again.

Revelation 21:4

Stepping Stones

Visualize Your Heavenly Reunion

- Open your favorite music app and play One Day by Cochren & Co. You can also choose any song that makes you feel all the feelings. Take time to visualize what you think heaven will be like and what you think your baby is doing there right now. Visualize how you think you'll react when you hear their voice or see them again. Since I love journaling so much, you get bonus points for writing all of this down. Tuck it away in a safe place where you can come back and read it whenever you need to.

8

Romans 8:18

"I consider that our present sufferings are not worth comparing with the glory that will be revealed in us."

I opened my Teen Study Bible for the second time that day, leafing through the pages in a search for…I wasn't sure. As I sifted through, the pages felt soft beneath my fingers—weathered from years of use in the past.

In high school, I thought I was close to God. I attended weekly church, and my friends and I were committed to studying His word outside of those Sunday mornings. But even while I gave my life to Christ in my teens, I now realize that I didn't fully understand the beauty of His work in my life. Up until that point, life was good, aside from a few teenage challenges we all faced.

It wasn't until I lost my son that I began to wrestle with God. In that wrestling, I truly began to feel Him move. Just like David in all of his grief, it was during the hard times when I felt God the most. But this didn't happen right away.

I would push Him away constantly, mostly because I was angry. But each time I felt angry with God, I also felt Him pull me into His word.

Unless you've felt this yourself, it's hard to describe. It was as if my broken heart created a vacuum that only His presence could fill. In my desperation to understand, to find meaning in the midst of chaos, I turned to His Word with a hunger I had never known.

As I sat in my living room and riffled through those old Bible pages from my youth, I smiled at some of the notes I'd written in the margins. I was naive then, as we all are as teenagers and young children. I probably thought at the time that if I continued to pray and glorify Him, He would never let anything bad happen to me.

I had a lot to learn.

And as I began to read, something began to shift within me. The words on the page weren't just ink anymore—they became a way of life. In the years since we lost Bodhi, I've read through the entire Bible four times. I'm currently on my fifth time through.

I don't say this to boast. I tell you this because each time, I've discovered new depths of God's love. Each time I've poured over the pages, I've found new facets of His character and new promises to cling to. It's as if my suffering was necessary for me to see the full glory of God with fresh eyes and an open heart.

Paul wrote the book of Romans to explain the gospel and encourage believers who were suffering for their faith. Chapter 8 is often considered the pinnacle of the letter, focusing on life in the Spirit and future glory. In it, Paul shows us that nothing can separate us from the love of God.

The Valley Between

When you initially read this specific verse, you may be tempted to feel a little roughness around the edges. This is especially true when it says, "Our present sufferings are not worth comparing…"

It's tough in the depths of grief to think about anything other than the suffering we're feeling. But Paul doesn't dismiss our current sufferings—he acknowledges them fully. He is offering a perspective that transcends our pain. He's lifting our eyes to a future so glorious it makes even our deepest sorrows wash away.

The encouraging thing I realized is that the glory Paul speaks of isn't only a far-off heavenly reward. It's something that God is working in us right now, through our sufferings. God is using every tear, every sleepless night, every moment of heartache to shape us, to refine us, to prepare us for a glory beyond our imagining.[IP]

And remember…we're unable, in our earthly bodies, to even imagine the plans that God could have for us. It's impossible.

As I write this, the pain of losing my son is still very real, still very sharp on some days. But through this experience and season of grief, God has revealed His glory. He's used my suffering to bring me closer to Him, and I've experienced a comfort that would never have been possible without it.

Now, this doesn't mean that I'm at all happy about having suffered through this loss. Given the choice, I would bring my son back in an instant, and I know that's true for you as well. But it does mean that I can look at my suffering through a different lens. I can see it as temporary, as a shadow that eventually gets swallowed up by the light of God's glory.

When I read this verse now, I imagine a set of weighing scales. On one side is all the pain, all the grief, all the suffering we experience in this life. It's heavy. It's unlike any other weight you could imagine.

On the other side is God's glory. It's the glory that will be revealed in us when we begin to surrender to Him. It's all the goodness that God is. While it seems like nothing could outweigh the weighty grief we see on side one, it's soon revealed that all it takes is God. Just as Paul said, our sufferings cannot compare to the weight of God's glory and goodness.

Years before having our first son, we struggled with infertility. I remember the pain and heartache so vividly. This was during a time when every single one of our friends was getting pregnant. There was no shortage of baby announcements popping into my social media feed.

The worst part? There was apparently no explanation for it, nothing in my body or my husband's that was preventing pregnancy from happening. It just wasn't.

So, while trying multiple treatments and medications and in an attempt to distract ourselves, my husband and I started an online company. Over the next few years, our company grew into something we could have never expected. It ultimately allowed us to live a life with complete time freedom, which is all I could have ever asked for. It allowed us to help thousands of people manage their dry eyes naturally and ultimately get their lives back.

But the business never would have happened had I become pregnant when we first started trying. We would have never dedicated the time it took to build and grow it. And it never would have completely changed the trajectory of our lives.

This is a great example of how God always has a plan that we cannot see. His plan is always good, even when it contains immense suffering and valleys of grief.

Now, I'm well aware that not everyone sees something big like this play out in their lives. But it doesn't have to be a big blessing for it to be a blessing we never saw coming.

Right now, I can imagine that your pain feels really heavy, and you might not feel very blessed. I know I felt the same way for a very long time. But remember, this doesn't end with suffering. Your story isn't going to end in pain and grief and loss. You have the opportunity to choose a different ending. This ending is full of glory, restoration, and potentially a blessing you never saw coming.

If you're in a place where suffering feels like all there is, I encourage you to hold onto this truth. Your pain is real, and it matters to God. But it's not the end of your story. There is a glory coming—a glory that's already at work in you. You just have to choose to let it draw you in.

Stepping Stones

Notice Unexpected Blessings

- Get out that trusty journal again (or any old sheet of paper). Think back on your life and remember a time when you experienced a blessing you never saw coming. This could be something big or something super small. Remember, blessings don't have to be big to be meaningful and make a positive impact on your life. Write it all down, and keep this in a place where you can easily reference it each time you need a reminder that this isn't the end of your story.

9

1 Thessalonians 4:13

"We do not want you to be uninformed about those who sleep in death, so that you do not grieve like the rest of mankind, who have no hope."

The crisp autumn air bit my cheeks as I sat with my friend in her backyard. Leaves of gold and orange drifted to the ground around us, a reminder of the changing seasons. We sat in comfortable silence for a while, sipping coffee and listening to the wind.

Then, my friend turned to me, her eyes filled with sadness. "You're so strong," she said, "I would never be able to endure what you did."

I felt a familiar tightness in my chest at her words. It wasn't the first time I'd heard this. After our loss, I had many people tell me how strong I was, how they couldn't imagine the pain. But the truth is, you will truly never know how strong you are until you are faced with challenges so heart-wrenching that you have no choice but to move forward through them.

Strength isn't something I naturally possess. I don't think of myself as brave or even confident most of the time. But after a loss like that, you have a choice. You can either choose to sludge forward, one step at a time, carrying your heavy backpack of grief along with you. Or you can choose to sit in your sorrow and remain stuck until you can no longer stay there. Eventually, we're all forced to move forward.

I chose early on to put my full trust in God and allow Him to give me the strength I needed to move forward. Did you catch that? It was and still is a choice. The strength people were seeing was not my own strength. It was God's strength shining through me.

"You could endure it," I replied gently. "Everyone can, even though no one should have to. You just don't realize it until something like this happens."

As I type these words, I'm reminded of 1 Thessalonians. Paul was encouraging the young church in Thessalonica, around 50-51 AD. These new believers were concerned about what happened to Christians who died before Christ's return. They worried that their deceased loved ones might miss out on Christ's second coming and resurrection.

This anxiety was causing deep distress in their community. This is not so far off from the distress you're probably feeling right now.

When Paul refers to those who "sleep", he's using a common euphemism for death that implies a temporary state. Like sleep, death for believers is not permanent.

The phrase "like the rest of mankind, who have no hope" is pretty significant here as well. In the ancient Greek and

Roman world, death was seen as final.⁶ They likely felt a complete hopelessness about seeing loved ones again.

But Paul is establishing a crucial difference here. Christian grief is fundamentally different because it's grounded in the hope of resurrection and reunion.

This doesn't mean Christians don't grieve deeply—Paul never suggests that. Instead, he's saying our grief is very different because of hope. For those who have lost babies, this verse offers particular comfort because it:

- Validates our grief while offering hope
- Promises reunion with our loved ones
- Assures us that death is temporary for believers
- Distinguishes between grief without hope and grief with eternal perspective

Grief is a natural, necessary response to loss, as we all know by now. But this verse reminds us that as believers, our grief is fundamentally different from those who do not believe.

We grieve, yes, but we grieve with hope that Christ will come again and that we will live for eternity with Him in heaven. Non-believers do not have this same hope.

As we've discussed in this section of the book, hope is where it's at. Jesus is where it's at. In those moments of your deepest pain and despair, He gives us the flicker of hope we

---

6   Department of Greek and Roman Art. "Death, Burial, and the Afterlife in Ancient Greece." In *Heilbrunn Timeline of Art History*. New York: The Metropolitan Museum of Art, October 2003. www.metmuseum.org/toah/hd/dbag/hd_dbag.htm. Accessed 5 March 2025.

need. He gives us the hope of reunion, the hope of eternal life, the hope that death is not the end of our story.

Paul is specifically saying he does not want you to be uninformed, and that means YOU, too! If you're uninformed about Jesus and everything God can do for your life, you're missing out on so much hope, love, and grace.

I tried to explain this to my friend. "It's not that I'm stronger than anyone else," I said. "It's that I'm holding onto a stronger hope. I know this suffering is temporary and there's a greater plan for my life."

The truth is, grief is universal. It touches every life at some point. You can't hide from it. You can't run from it. But hope? Hope is a choice. It's a gift offered to everyone through Christ, but we have to choose to accept it, to cling to it even when our feelings try to tell us otherwise. We have to seek Him even on days when we're angry or sad.

Now, this doesn't mean we don't feel the weight of our loss in those moments. It doesn't mean we just put a smile on our face to please others or pretend everything is fine. Rather, it means we acknowledge how much it hurts while also holding onto the promise of a future where our pain is healed.

So, if you're reading this and you're thinking, "I don't even know God," remember that you have a choice to make. You can choose to move forward without hope and try to carry this grief all on your own. But it's a heavy load to carry.

Alternatively, you can remember that you have access to never-ending hope and choose to lean into God's call. In doing so, you'll grieve not as someone who pushes hope away but as someone who embraces it. You'll have Jesus by your side, lightening your load.

As Christians, we do not grieve as those who have no hope. We grieve as those who know an empty tomb lies beyond the cross. Beyond death lies resurrection. Beyond our present suffering lies a glory that will make all things new.

Stepping Stones

Say Yes to Hope

- As we come to the end of this section on hope, I'd like to invite you to give your life to Jesus by praying the following prayer. This prayer comes from Adventure Church, which we attend, and I believe it's a beautiful way to give your life to Him.[7] If you've already done so, this is still a great prayer to recite to remind yourself to whom you belong. If you're not quite ready, that's ok too. This book and prayer will always be a resource for you whenever you need it.

    Dear Jesus, today I invite you in. Come into my life, forgive me of my sin. I believe that you're the Son of God, that you died for me so that I can live for you. I surrender all that I am to You and Your plan. In Jesus' name, Amen.

---

[7] Visit Adventure.Church for more information

PART IV

God's Strength in the Valley

Years ago, it was normal for children to be raised by not only their parents but also their grandparents, great grandparents, aunts, uncles, cousins, friends, and neighbors. This is still true in some countries today, and there's so much beauty and strength in that.

We were never meant to do life alone. But the busyness of our schedules and our hustle mentality often lead us to ignore how much we need help. We think we can do it alone. We can do it better than anyone else. We don't need help.

But when grief knocks us to our knees, it's often there that we discover this great truth: We were never meant to stand alone. In our weakest moments, when our own strength fails us, God's strength becomes most evident. It's not about being strong enough. This is about recognizing that His strength is sufficient when ours is not.

I learned this lesson in the most vulnerable season of my life, when fear and joy collided in an unexpected way. Just months after losing our son, I discovered I was pregnant again with baby boy number three.

The news that should have brought pure joy instead brought a complex mixture of emotions. I felt hope tangled with fear, excitement woven with anxiety, and gratitude overshadowed by grief. In this season, I truly learned what it meant to lean into God's strength rather than my own.

I know this section may be tough for some of you to read. The loss of your baby may still be very fresh in your mind, and even hearing of someone else becoming pregnant may be triggering. If that's true for you, don't hesitate to set this book down and come back to it later.

Alternatively, if you feel up to it, we're about to embark on the next trail of this journey through grief. If you're an anxious person like me, it may challenge you. But it's going to give you a beautiful perspective filled with hope, grace, and a strength like you will never know on your own.

10

Philippians 4:6-7

> "Do not be anxious about anything, but in every situation, by prayer and petition, with thanksgiving, present your requests to God. And the peace of God, which transcends all understanding, will guard your hearts and your minds in Christ Jesus."

The pregnancy test sat on the counter, two pink lines clearly visible. My hands trembled as I stared at it, my heart racing with a thousand emotions. I started to sweat. Just months after saying goodbye, here I was, carrying another precious life. The joy I felt was immediate, but so was the fear.

Every mother who has experienced loss knows this fear, whether you've had a pregnancy after your loss or not. It's the fear that history might repeat itself, that joy might once again be snatched away.

Even in the early months after our loss, this fear consumed me when I thought about every little bad thing that could happen to our oldest. What if he ran across the street and got hit by a car? What if someone snatched him from the playground? What if something happened to him at daycare, and I wasn't there to help? The fear was palpable.

As I stood there in the bathroom, I felt this same fear threatening to overwhelm me. But then, I remembered this verse from Philippians. This is my favorite verse in the Bible because, let's be honest, I need it most. If I were ever to get a verse tattooed on my body, this would be it.

"Do not be anxious about anything…"

But how could I not be anxious? I had just lost a child. I worried about losing our oldest every single minute of his life. Now, I had another son to be worried about. The wounds were still fresh, the grief still very raw. And yet, here was God's Word, offering not just a command but a promise to "guard (my) heart."

When Paul wrote these verses, he was in prison, yet he penned what's known as his most joyful letter. This context is crucial because he's teaching about peace from a place of personal hardship. He was fearful and anxious, just like you probably are today.

The passage offers a clear formula for dealing with anxiety while promising peace in return. Here's the formula:

Pray about everything + petition/present your requests to God + give thanks for everything = peace.

It's significant that thanksgiving is included even in our moments of distress. This suggests that gratitude also plays a key role in receiving God's peace. It's not just prayers and asking God for help. It's important to also be thankful for what He's given us, both the good and the bad.

We remind our kids all the time that they can get more of what they want in life by appreciating what they have. If they're whining about a toy at Target that they have to have,

I remind them of the last time I saw them play with a similar toy. More often than not, they haven't touched this toy in months.

Being thankful for what you have—whether it's toys or a roof over your head—is one part of the peace formula for a reason. Without thanksgiving for all that God has done, we will never know true peace in our lives.

So I knew I had a choice to make, just like Paul did. I could either let anxiety consume me for the next nine months or I could lean into God's strength and trust His plan. There wasn't room for both.

While I knew those nine months wouldn't be easy, I made a conscious decision to rest in God's strength rather than my own. Each day of my pregnancy became an exercise in surrender.

Our twenty-week ultrasound was incredibly daunting since it was at our last one that we found out Bodhi's life would be brief. Thankfully, all was well, but as we got closer to our son's due date, I needed God more than ever.

I was no longer naive. I no longer thought that pregnancy equals a healthy baby. I knew too many people who had lost their babies right up to their due dates or shortly after.

So I turned to His Word. I turned to prayer. Sometimes, these prayers were faith-filled. Other times, they were desperate, blubbering cries for Him to protect this baby because I couldn't. Each time I had the thought that I could lose this baby too, I started talking to God. I practiced giving everything hard to Him.

Now is also a great time for me to mention that I found a wonderful therapist during this time. She was instrumental in allowing me to fully process my grief and the emotions I was feeling. Without Jesus and a bit of counseling, I'm not sure how I could have made it through those nine months.

It's normal to feel completely hopeless, angry, and even guilty after losing your baby. It's normal to not want to leave your house for fear of triggers. But if it's been a couple of months and you're still confined to your home or having destructive thoughts, please get outside help. This may be therapy, or it may be medication. Do what you need to do to move forward towards peace.

The peace that I eventually felt wasn't always constant. Since I struggle with anxiety and fear daily, peace would only pop in every once in a while. But it was enough for me. Sometimes it was a quiet whisper, and other times it was a strong presence that carried me through difficult doctor's appointments or sleepless nights.

Peace is always able to peek through if you let it in, if you give your anxieties and fears to God.

What I learned during this pregnancy was that God's peace isn't only a warm and fuzzy feeling. His peace can actually act as a guard for our hearts in those tough moments. When we bring our anxieties to Him, when we choose to trust Him instead of our fears, His peace stands watch over our hearts and minds. It doesn't mean we won't feel afraid or worried, but it means those feelings don't get to have the final say. They don't get to be in the driver's seat of our lives.

If you're anxious today, whether it's about another pregnancy, whether or not you can get pregnant again, your other kiddos, or anything else, let this be an encouragement for you. Know that I am praying for you. I'm praying for you as I type this—that you would surrender your fears and anxieties to God.

Let Him take the lead and guard your heart so you can live the beautiful life He intended for you. He doesn't expect us to be fearless on our own. This is impossible. He simply

Philippians 4:6-7

asks us to bring our fears to Him and to let Him carry the burdens that are too heavy for us.

During this pregnancy, I developed a few practical ways to combat my anxiety and fear. Feel free to use some or all of these ideas if you're feeling ambitious:

1. **Morning Surrenders:** Each morning, I would place my hand on my stomach and surrender that day to God. "Lord, this baby is yours. This day is yours. I trust you." You can use any prayer that feels good to you.

2. **Scripture Cards:** I wrote verses and prayers about peace and God's faithfulness on index cards. I then placed them in a special box on my nightstand. When anxiety would strike, I would read them aloud. Many of those verses you'll find in this book.

3. **Gratitude Moments:** Even in my fear, I would thank God for specific things about the pregnancy or my life in general. "Thank you for another day with this baby. Thank you for each kick and movement." You can also do this by keeping a gratitude journal near your bed. Each night, write down three things you're grateful for. The results might surprise you.

4. **Community Prayers:** I shared my fears with trusted friends and family members. They would pray with and for me, reminding me that I wasn't walking this journey alone. If you don't feel like you have anyone who can be a support for you, seek out a Bible study group, church group, or online support group you can become a part of.

Strength isn't found in the absence of fear but in knowing where to turn when fear comes. It's found in the daily choice to trust God's plan over our anxieties, to lean into His strength when ours fails, and to believe that His peace is stronger than our fears. You've got this.

Stepping Stones

Give it to God

- Practice morning surrenders (or bedtime surrenders, whichever one fits into your schedule more easily). This only takes a few seconds, but it's a great way to feel closer to God and the baby you've lost. Surrender that day to God, saying, "Lord, this day is yours. Help me live my life through your will, your way. I trust you. Amen." You can use this prayer or another one that feels good to you.

11

Isaiah 41:10

"So do not fear, for I am with you; do not be dismayed, for I am your God. I will strengthen you and help you; I will uphold you with my righteous right hand."

This seems like a great time to explore the difference between fear and anxiety, so let's do it. While fear and anxiety are often used interchangeably, they are distinctly different experiences, especially in the context of grief and loss.

Fear is a God-given emotion with a specific trigger or threat, serving as our natural protective response. It is often focused on the present or something currently threatening (like a loud noise or your child darting into the street).

Anxiety, on the other hand, often lacks a specific trigger and is more future-oriented, producing an ongoing state of worry. Often, there's no explanation for anxiety aside from it being a figment of your imagination. As you can imagine, this can become overwhelming for those who suffer from it.

Although we often use these words interchangeably, scripture addresses both emotions differently. Fear appears throughout the Bible, and we're often told to fear not or to not be afraid. It's often related to specific situations like David versus Goliath or Moses leading his people.

Anxiety, however, is often used to speak of ongoing concerns about the future. In this way, anxiety encompasses a longer road and often sticks around for the long haul.

In the context of pregnancy and infant loss, fear might manifest as specific concerns. These may include fear of forgetting your baby, fear of another loss, or fear of particular triggers or dates. Anxiety, however, shows up as a general worry about the future, persistent unease about pregnancy, or constant "what if" scenarios we make up in our heads.

I include this specific verse in this book because it is so powerful, and it contains clear commands and promises from God. The book of Isaiah is full of prophecies and promises, especially those involving the coming of Christ. It was written for people who were frightened and uncertain about the future, similar to how you're probably feeling right now.

Isaiah was one of the major prophets in the Old Testament, and he did his fair share of writing what he experienced from God. The world was rough at that time, but Isaiah came through with many beautiful promises about hope.

This specific verse contains five distinct promises that God makes to His people:

1. He commands them not to fear, but this isn't a harsh command—it's coupled with the tender reminder, "For I am with you."

2. He tells them not to be dismayed (or anxious) because He is their God.

Isaiah 41:10

3. He will strengthen them.
4. He will help them.
5. He will uphold them with His righteous right hand.

The imagery of God's "right hand" is significant in Hebrew culture, representing His power, authority, and ability to save. Also, the final three promises are active on God's part. He will do all this *for* us because we are His children.

In my discussions with other loss mamas, one of the biggest fears that comes up is the fear of another loss. We all know how heart-wrenching this situation is. We know how devastating it is to carry this grief with us throughout our lives. Yet, we often still yearn for another baby within the real fear of losing said baby. While we may want that rainbow baby so badly, we may even fear trying to get pregnant in the first place.

I know I felt this way immediately after I found out I was pregnant again, which I discussed in the last chapter. Although I didn't ever fear trying to get pregnant again, the fear of actually being pregnant again was very real.

If you're feeling anxiety around your next pregnancy or the thought of it, you are not alone. And if you're at the point where you've decided not to try for another baby (or maybe you can't), I know there's a ton of anxiety around that as well. You may be wondering what life will look like moving forward. I want you to know that your fears and anxieties are all valid, and they're all very normal responses to loss.

After pregnancy or infant loss, we all have fear and anxiety. If you're anything like me, you struggle with trusting God in the midst of this hurt. But that's exactly what we need to try to do. If you're dealing with fear around a specific situation today, here are a few promises you can remember. Put them on sticky notes around your house, write them in your journal or planner, and say them out loud when you're feeling extra fearful:

1. Do not fear, for God is with you
2. Do not be anxious, for God is for you
3. God will strengthen you and help you
4. God will uphold you with his righteous right hand

In addition to this, you can always pull truth from any of the verses highlighted in this book. Here are a few other verses that may be helpful when you're dealing with fear:

- **Jeremiah 29:11** - "For I know the plans I have for you," declares the Lord, "Plans to prosper you and not to harm you, plans to give you hope and a future."
- **2 Corinthians 12:9** - But he said to me, "My grace is sufficient for you, for my power is made perfect in weakness." Therefore, I will boast all the more gladly about my weaknesses, so that Christ's power may rest on me.

There are many more you could use since the Bible is filled with God's great promises for us. Through the fear, anxiety, and loss, this truth remains constant—God is always good. God is always for us.

This is not only true when things go according to our plans, but it's also true when you're wondering where God is in your plans. It's true when you've experienced so much loss and hurt that you're wondering if He really is for you.

His goodness doesn't depend on our circumstances. His goodness is woven through every little experience we go through in life, both the joyful and the hurtful.

Isaiah 41:10

When God commands us, "Do not fear, for I am with you," He's reminding us that His presence is our security. He never promises that our life will be free from pain. In fact, He tells us we'll have plenty of difficult times as believers. But He does promise that, through it all, He will be right there with us to strengthen us, walk with us, and lead us through our pain into whatever He has planned for us next.

No matter what fear you're facing today (and there may be many), try to remember that He is always good. His plans are always good and always have your best interest at heart. Whether your path is clear or muddled with grief, whether your arms are full or aching with emptiness, He promises to be with you and lead you through it. This awful journey doesn't get the final say because God always does.

Stepping Stones

Remind Yourself Who He Is

- We all need a little encouragement that God is always for us. Use the following personal statements to remind yourself who He is. Put them on sticky notes around your house, write them in your journal or planner, and say them out loud when you're feeling extra fearful:

  - Do not fear, for God is with me
  - Do not be anxious, for God is for me
  - God will strengthen me and help me
  - God will uphold me with his righteous right hand

12

John 16:33

> "I have told you these things, so that in me you may have peace. In this world you will have trouble. But take heart! I have overcome the world."

It took years for me to get to this point. As I sit here in my tiny basement office, faint light creeping through the window, I can finally say that I have made peace with my son being gone. I no longer feel the constant weight and pressure of grief around me. I no longer feel like I'm carrying a heavy pack that's weighing me down every single moment of my life.

Most days are good, busy, and full of love. Some days are still really tough. Bodhi would be five this weekend. If he were with us on Earth today, he'd be in pre-K, making friends and making trouble with his brothers. I'd be sending him off to Kindergarten in a few months.

And while I have an overall sense of peace around this situation, it's because of those thoughts that grief is still there.

When we lose someone we love so much, we don't just grieve for that moment. We grieve for every little moment we don't get to experience with them here on Earth.

Hearing their first word. Putting them on the school bus for the first time. Watching them play with their siblings. Cheering for them in the stands as they score their first goal or walk across the stage at graduation. Dancing with them at their wedding…

These are all life experiences we wish we could have with them, and these longings are unavoidable. This is why grief never fully goes away. Grief is the proof that you love your baby so fiercely, and you always will. This is why you have to pick it up and carry it with you. It will evolve and change over time, just like many things, but its presence will always be there.

The important truth I've come to know is that grief and peace can coexist. We can eventually find an overall sense of peace in our lives while also grieving each of the little moments we miss with them gone.

When we lost our son shortly before Christmas, I knew it would be a difficult season for us. Grief and pain interspersed with joy and Christmas carols. I wasn't feeling particularly jolly, but I chose to put up our decorations in early November that year.

I bought him a stocking to match the rest of our family, and I put up all of the angel ornaments people had gifted to us. I was grasping for any little joy I could find because I knew I needed it so much. If you're in a place where finding joy seems impossible, that's ok too.

We worked with Sufficient Grace Ministries, a bereavement support service,[8] after our son's diagnosis and while in

---

[8] SufficientGraceMinistries.org

the hospital, so I knew they made memory ornaments for babies lost. I've ordered one every year since, and I'm soon going to need a separate tree for them.

I did all of this during that hard season in my life, and I continue to do these things to this day. This is just one of the ways I allow grief and peace to coexist. I'm acknowledging that my son is gone but also knowing that he lived inside me. Holidays can be incredibly hard after you've lost a baby, so I encourage you to include your little one in the seasons and holidays that mean the most to you.

This could mean getting a stocking for them that you hang every year, ordering an ornament for them, or writing them a letter each year on Christmas. Including them will help you bring joy and peace into a situation that seems to be anything but.

We do the same for my son's birthday. We get cake and ice cream, bring one of his photos out, and sing him Happy Birthday. If you don't have a specific birthday for your baby, choose a date that is meaningful for you and do something special on their day.

When Jesus spoke these words in John 16, He was preparing His disciples for His death. He knew the pain they would face, just as He knows the pain we face today. Notice He doesn't promise a trouble-free life—quite the opposite. Jesus explicitly tells his disciples that they *will* have trouble. But He offers something more valuable: His peace in the midst of it.

Both trouble and peace. Trouble, but peace in the midst of it.

Just because we feel peace doesn't mean there is no more grief.[IP] Just because we feel peace doesn't mean we stop missing our babies. Peace is simply the understanding that our story doesn't end here, and their story doesn't end with their death.

John 16:33

When Jesus says, "I have overcome the world," He's reminding us that earthly loss isn't the final word. Our children are in the presence of the One who has overcome everything—even death.

We've discussed this before, but I think it's important to point it out again. Unfortunately, many people were raised (even in Christian households) to believe that God does not want us to feel negative feelings. But that is so far from the truth. We know this because Jesus is God, and Jesus knew what it was like to grieve.

He wept at Lazarus's tomb even knowing He would raise him from the dead. He very often took time by himself to be with God and with His feelings. He understands our tears and our questions because He's experienced it all. When He promises peace, it's not some superficial band-aid, but it is a source of deep comfort for us that is always there if we allow it to be.

This is the kind of peace I've found. It's not a peace that erases the reality of loss but one that transforms how I carry it. Yes, I still miss my son every single day. I think about him every single day. And I still wonder about all the moments we'll miss without him on Earth.

But I also have peace knowing he is experiencing something far greater than anything this world could offer. Every milestone he's missing here, he's experiencing something more beautiful in heaven. There's still grief, but I am at peace.

Your journey may look very different from mine. You may read this and think, "It took her five years to find peace with this?" or "I'll never find peace like that." But no matter your story or the type of person you are, peace is possible if you let Jesus in to help you fully process the pain you're experiencing.

He gives us permission to miss our babies while also holding onto the hope of reunion. He allows us to acknowledge the weight of our loss while trusting that he's overcome the world, including the pain and death itself.

As you navigate your own journey, remember that you don't need to choose between the two. Grief and peace can coexist in a beautiful way. You can miss your baby fiercely while also knowing this isn't the end.

I'll encourage you to acknowledge the milestones you're missing while holding onto the promise of eternity. If you're not already reading your Bible, now is the time to crack it open. (Or buy one if you need to!) If you're not sure where to turn, start with some of the verses you've read in this book and start reading.

Let Him pour into you, and I guarantee the weight of your pain will soon begin to feel just a little bit lighter.

Stepping Stones

Include Your Baby

- Whether it's close to a holiday or not, think of ways you can include them in the next one. This might mean buying them a stocking and displaying it every year, getting them an ornament, buying a birthday cake, or writing them a letter on a holiday that's special for you and your family. Including your baby in your life, no matter how brief their life was, is a special way to keep their memory alive. It's also a great way to find peace in the darkest valley of grief.

PART V
Finding Purpose in the Depths

There comes a moment in every grief journey when we begin to see light breaking through the darkness. Not because our loss hurts less or because we've "moved on," but because God begins to reveal purpose even in our deepest pain. This transformation doesn't happen overnight. It's gradual, like dealing with grief itself. For me, this process took years to unfold.

When we first lose a baby, the idea of finding purpose in our pain seems impossible, maybe even cruel. It's the last thing we want to think about. We never want to hear, "Everything happens for a reason," or "It was just meant to be," or "Your baby is in a better place." We all know that these are terrible things to say to someone whose world has just crashed down on them.

How could there be any purpose in empty arms and the loss of someone we love so much? In those early days, we're simply trying to survive. We're trying to breathe through the next moment, to somehow keep putting one foot in front of the other. And that's okay. That's exactly where we need to be in those moments.

But as time passes, something begins to shift. I never thought I would begin to feel normal, but time is a great healer. The raw edges of grief, while never completely smooth, begin to take on new meaning.

After a while of walking through the dark valley of my grief, I began to notice a little light breaking through the clouds. I began to notice how my experience had changed me—not just in my pain but in my capacity for compassion. I was able to empathize with others' suffering, and I had the ability to sit with someone in their hardest moments and say, "I understand. You're not alone."

If you've been through a loss like this, you know exactly how it feels to lose your greatest love. You know how it feels to lose a piece of your heart that you can never get back while here on Earth. You truly do understand what others are going through, and there's a ton of beauty in that.

This section isn't about "getting over" your loss or finding a silver lining in tragedy. Instead, it's about discovering how God can weave purpose into our pain and hope into our heartbreak. He can heal all things in a beautiful way. He's done it for me, and I believe He will do it for you, too.

This section of our journey is about seeing how our stories, as painful as they are, can become a light of hope for others walking similar paths. In Matthew 5, God tells us not to let our light be hidden. Instead, He encourages us to "Let your light shine before others."

The journey from deep, heavy grief to finding purpose isn't linear.[IP] Some days, you'll feel strong enough to reach out and help others. Other days, you'll need to step back and tend to your own healing. Both are valid. Both are necessary. Both are part of how God works through your story.

13

Romans 8:28

"And we know that in all things God works for the good of those who love him, who have been called according to his purpose."

Sometimes, God's calling comes as a whisper, a gentle nudge that's easy to dismiss. That's how it started for me—a quiet thought about writing a book about my grief experience "someday."

But God's whispers have a way of becoming impossible to ignore, especially when they're born from our deepest wounds.

I began to feel the gentle nudge to write this book a few years ago. It was just a thought at first, and it was something I never truly thought I would have the courage to do. This was fairly early on in my grief journey—within the first few months after my loss. The thought would come into my mind, and I would quickly swipe it aside.

I definitely wasn't ready. Would I ever be ready?

I had a lot going on in my life at that time, raising my oldest son and working with my husband on our business. At the time, I didn't feel like I had the time to tackle something so big. I knew this was something that could potentially be very meaningful and helpful for people who were struggling. I wanted to do it right.

For years, I pushed aside the idea of even sitting down to start. After all, who was I to speak into other women's grief? What could I possibly say that would make a difference? I didn't feel adequate.

Grief is a messy thing, and everyone is different. I was afraid I wouldn't have the right words to say or that I would offend someone with my story. Looking back, this was all due to fear of the unknown and my anxiety creeping in.

But the calling persisted, growing stronger until it became impossible to ignore. A few months ago, I started seeing grief everywhere: on social media, with friends of friends, and in random conversations. This seemed different than at the beginning, where you notice it because that's all you're thinking about.

The reticular activating system (RAS) in your brain is the reason you tend to notice things you're actively thinking about.[9] This is like seeing tons of red cars on the road when you've been thinking about buying one.

I'm not sure whether it was my RAS at work or simply God, but it had been a while since I had thought about my grief. It had been a while since I had actively researched it or sought out other people going through the same thing.

---

[9] "Your Brain at Work: The Reticular Activating System (RAS) and Your Goals & Behaviour." *Life Exchange*. 2025. https://lifexchangesolutions.com/reticular-activating-system. Accessed 5 March 2025.

It's funny how God works. He often uses our deepest pain as the very thing that enables us to help others, and I believe He was working on this in me.

I decided to sit down at my computer and start writing what I felt in my heart needed to be shared. I was doing this for me and me alone, or so I thought. I woke up one morning and knew exactly how I should structure the book.

I sat down to write that morning, and the words poured out of me. I couldn't stop typing, and it was as if someone was guiding my fingers and my mind. The words came so easily, and I knew this was nothing other than God at work in me and through me.

Now, let me be clear about the specific verse I've highlighted for this chapter. This verse from Romans isn't suggesting that everything that happens is good or that there is a reason for everything that happens. The loss of our babies isn't good. The heartache isn't good. The empty arms and shattered dreams aren't good. God is not the creator of our problems, but He is the creator of all that is good.

I think it's important to distinguish between there being a "reason" for your loss and a "purpose." There's a significant difference between saying "there's a reason for everything" and finding purpose through our pain. The first implies that God caused our loss for some specific reason, which can be both theologically problematic and deeply hurtful.

The idea of "everything happens for a reason" suggests that God actively chose to take our babies from us to teach us something or make something happen. This view can make God seem cruel and can lead to harmful questions. "What did I do wrong?" or "Why is God punishing me?"

However, finding purpose through our pain is different. This perspective acknowledges that while God didn't cause our loss, He can work through it to bring about something meaningful.

God, in His infinite wisdom and love, can work through our painful circumstances to create purpose and meaning and so much beauty. He will absolutely use the hardships in our lives to bring us closer to Him. He wants to transform us into people who are more like Him. That should be the entire goal of our lives, after all.

When we first lose a baby, talking about "purpose" in our pain feels impossible, maybe even offensive or heartless. But as time passes, and as we allow God to work in and through our grief, we begin to see how He can use our story to bring hope to others walking the same path.

Remember, you are not alone. There have been many women who have gone before you, and there will be many women after who will become part of this same awful club we never asked to join.

Writing this book isn't a way for me to move past my grief or get over the loss of my son. We all know by now that that will never happen. But it does allow God to use my experience—every tear, every question, every moment of anger and doubt—to reach out to other mothers (you!) who feel alone in their loss. Grief changes us forever, but it doesn't have to destroy us.

This is what Romans 8:28 means when it talks about God working for good. He doesn't cause our pain, but He can use it. He doesn't erase our loss, but He can give it purpose. He doesn't take away our grief, but He can transform it into a tool for helping others.

Maybe you're reading this and thinking, "I don't see any purpose in my pain, and I never will." That's okay. I was right there with you for a very long time. You don't have to see it right now.

Sometimes, the purpose doesn't become clear until years later, and sometimes, we won't understand it until we reach heaven. I know this is hard to hear, but I'm not sure all of us will know the purpose of our loss here on Earth.

For example, some people will be called to share their grief publicly. They may see many people transform their lives and give their lives to God. On the other hand, you may have a conversation about your story with a stranger who is hurting. You may never find out how their life turned out until you reach heaven. But maybe it was your story that was the turning point in their lives.

This is something I've struggled with, but what I do know is that we can trust that God is at work, even when we can't see it. Your story matters. Your baby's life matters. And while you might not be able to see it yet, God can use your journey—every part of it—for good.

Sharing your story and finding purpose in it will never minimize your loss, but it does have the potential to multiply its meaning. This will not erase your grief, but it will expand its purpose. A purpose will never replace your baby, but it might reach others through the love you feel for your child.

The purpose might look different for each of us. For some, it might be starting a support group. For others, it might be becoming a shoulder to cry on for other loss moms. Or maybe, like me, it might be writing about your experience. Whatever form it takes, know that God can use your story in beautiful ways.

Remember, you don't have to force this. You don't have to search for purpose or manufacture meaning. Remain open to how God might want to use your experience to help others. Sometimes, the most powerful ministry comes from simply being willing to share your story and sit with others in their pain.

The purpose God reveals through our pain often looks different than we might expect. Sometimes, it's as quiet as being able to sit with another grieving mother and truly understand her heart.

Sometimes, it's as public as starting a ministry or writing a book. Sometimes, it's simply being willing to say our baby's name and share their story. This is so important because it helps to break the silence that too often surrounds pregnancy and infant loss.

When we look at Scripture, we see this pattern again and again—God uses people's deepest pain for profound purposes. Here are a few examples:

Joseph

- Sold into slavery by his brothers
- Falsely imprisoned
- Separated from his family for decades
- Yet became second-in-command of Egypt and saved many lives, including his family
- **Key verse: Genesis 50:20** - "You intended to harm me, but God intended it for good to accomplish what is now being done, the saving of many lives."

Job

- Lost his children, wealth, and health all at once
- Experienced deep depression and questioning
- Yet his story has comforted suffering people for generations

- Later in his life, everything was restored in a way that only God could do
- **Key verse: Job 42:5** - "My ears had heard of you, but now my eyes have seen you."

David

- Experienced betrayal, loss of children, exile
- His raw grief and pain became the Psalms
- His honest expressions of both sorrow and hope have guided believers through grief for centuries
- **Key verse: Psalm 30:5** - "Weeping may stay for the night, but rejoicing comes in the morning."

Naomi and Ruth

- Both widowed and bereft
- Left their homeland alone
- Their story of loss led to being in the lineage of Jesus
- **Key verse: Ruth 4:14-15** - "Praise be to the Lord, who this day has not left you without a guardian-redeemer…"

Hannah

- Experienced years of infertility and mockery
- Her pain led to deep prayer

- Became mother to Samuel, one of Israel's greatest prophets
- **Key verse: 1 Samuel 2:1** - "My heart rejoices in the Lord..."

There are so many others I could have highlighted here. He has a great purpose for your life as well. Even Jesus's own suffering served the greatest purpose of all—our redemption.

God did not cause our losses. He didn't want our babies to die. But He *can* take even our deepest, darkest pain and use it to bring hope to others. He can use it to draw us closer to Him, closer to others on the same path, and to create beauty from ashes.

For me, the purpose began to reveal itself in unexpected ways. It showed up in passing thoughts, conversations with other loss moms, and things I noticed people struggling with in online support groups and through prayer.

Although your pain may look different from mine, it's still the same feeling of loss. It's the loss of one of the greatest loves in your life. It's the loss of a piece of you.

Eventually, purpose manifested when I realized I couldn't hold my story in any longer. I couldn't hold back God's love any longer. This book is a calling that started as a whisper and grew into an undeniable pull to share hope with others walking this path. To share hope with *you*.

Your purpose might look different. Perhaps God will use your story to:

- Start a support group for grieving parents
- Become a shoulder to cry on for others experiencing loss

- Create art that expresses the inexpressible
- Advocate for better support for families experiencing loss
- Work with families as a bereavement doula
- Be willing to share your story with someone who needs to hear they're not alone

Whatever form it takes, know that your pain isn't purposeless. Your baby's life, no matter how brief, has meaning. And while we might not understand the full picture on this side of heaven, we can trust that God is working all things—even our deepest hurts—for good.

This doesn't minimize our loss. It doesn't make the pain disappear. But it does give us hope that our stories don't end in grief. They continue in purpose, in meaning, in bringing light to others walking through this valley of darkness.

Stepping Stones

Ask for Next Steps

- Start praying to God and asking Him to reveal the next steps for you. Pray for clarity around your situation and for healing to occur so that you're able to use your story to bless others. This does not need to be anything fancy. The exact wording doesn't matter here, but your intent does. I prayed a similar prayer for a very long time before I felt God move. But if you consistently do this, I believe He will direct the next step for where He wants you to go.

14

Psalm 30:5

"Weeping may stay for the night, but rejoicing comes in the morning."

David didn't have it easy. He was overlooked, doubted, and experienced devastating loss and betrayal. Yet through everything, he stayed firm to his description as a man after God's own heart.

When David wrote Psalm 30, he was dedicating the new temple—likely after a period of intense trial. The psalm was written as a song of thanksgiving, acknowledging how God had pulled him up from the depths of despair.

David knew what it meant to weep through the night. He had experienced the deaths of his children, faced betrayal, and walked through valleys of deep sadness. Yet he also knew the faithfulness of God to bring joy after mourning.

This verse uses imagery that would have resonated with the society David was living in at the time. In ancient times, night was a period of particular vulnerability. It was a time of danger, uncertainty, and often weeping. It sounds a lot like grief! But morning always came, bringing light, hope, and new beginnings.

The Hebrew word for "stay" suggests a temporary lodging, while "rejoicing" implies a shout of celebration. David is telling us that sorrow may take up residence in our lives, but it's not a permanent tenant. It's temporary. And joy? It will come, and we're meant to celebrate it when it does.

Just like the devastation of your loss, the deep sorrow will definitely be around for a while. But it's not permanent. Your grief will change, ebbing and flowing throughout the rest of your life. It will ultimately mold you into someone more similar to Jesus himself. This is God's plan.

[TRIGGER WARNING: Discussion of subsequent pregnancy and birth]

I already touched on this subject a bit earlier, but I wanted to dive a little deeper. I experienced the truth of this psalm most powerfully during the pregnancy and the birth of our youngest son. If you've ever experienced pregnancy after loss, you'll know that it's filled with immense fear and uncertainty.

Each doctor's appointment and milestone brought both hope and trepidation. This is normal. Our hearts remember our losses, and fear becomes a familiar companion on this journey. Would the same thing happen again? Am I going to lose this baby, too?

Throughout those nine months, I understood David's language of weeping in the night. There were countless moments of anxiety, of wondering if morning would ever come. But like David, I also learned about God's faithfulness in those dark hours.

He showed me that joy and grief could coexist. He showed me that I could be devastated about the loss of our son yet also be excited about my pregnancy with our next one. Two things are true here, and I believe this can be true for everyone.

When labor began, it was swift and intense. My water broke at 2:00 PM, and for three hours, I prayed with the same desperate hope that marks many of David's psalms: "Lord, let us hear his cry. Let him be safe. Let my baby be alive."

At 5:00 PM, those prayers were answered with our son's first cry. I felt instant relief. He was very purple and bruised from the quick birth, and he needed some oxygen, but he was perfect.

So here's what's important to understand about this psalm and this situation: David's joy in the morning didn't erase his memories of weeping. Similarly, the joy of holding our youngest son has never erased the grief of losing his brother.

He isn't a replacement—no child ever could be. Rather, his life stands as a testament to God's faithfulness, a reminder that joy can return even after the deepest sorrow.

This is what David understood when he wrote about joy coming in the morning. He wasn't promising that our grief would end or that we'd forget what we've lost. Instead, he was testifying to God's faithfulness to bring light after darkness. Remember, God is always working for good because He is good.

As you walk through this valley between who you once were and who you are becoming, God is with you. I know it sucks, and I know that you never asked for any of this. But He is there, and He is good.

Your "morning" might look different than David's or mine. It might not be another baby. You may have decided that trying again isn't for you. You may not be able to have more children. You may continue to experience loss with or without any reason for it.

But your morning could also mean finding purpose in helping others, discovering new depths in your faith, or experiencing moments of unexpected joy that surprise you with their intensity. Whatever form it takes, the promise remains: weeping may stay for a night (however long that night may be), but joy will come with the morning.

This truth doesn't invalidate our grief or suggest we should move on. We both know that's impossible. Instead, like David, we can hold both our sorrow and our hope, our weeping and our joy, knowing that they tell the full story of God's faithfulness in our lives.

He sees our tears, remembers our losses, and promises to bring light into our darkness. Just as He brings morning sunshine after a hard night, there will be redemption. God is working in your life, and He's working it for good.

Stepping Stones

Invite Joy In

- Today, I'd like you to do something that brings you joy. I want to show you that both joy and grief can coexist in a beautiful way. This can be something small, like getting a pedicure or watching your favorite funny movie. It could also be something bigger, like volunteering at a local soup kitchen or thrift store. Whatever you love to do, be it for yourself or someone else, take time to do that thing today. Notice the joy you feel, and try not to feel guilty for allowing a small amount of joy to exist amidst your pain.

15

2 Corinthians 4:18

"So we fix our eyes not on what is seen,
but on what is unseen, since what is seen is temporary,
but what is unseen is eternal."

In the early days after losing our son, I had a hard time knowing where to turn. I came across this verse during one of the hardest nights of my life. I missed our son so badly—with my entire body. I could feel it in my bones. I felt his absence so intensely.

I had snuck out of our bedroom and opened my Bible to start reading. This verse was right there, the first one I read.

When all I could see was emptiness—empty arms, empty bedroom, empty future—this verse reminded me to look beyond what my eyes were physically seeing to what my heart could believe.

When Paul wrote these words to the Corinthian church, he was addressing believers facing persecution and suffering.

Just verses earlier, he describes being "hard pressed on every side" and "perplexed." He understood what it meant to fix his eyes on eternal hope when present circumstances felt unbearable.

The Greek word for "fix our eyes" (skopeō) means to look intently at something, to focus with purpose and concentration. It's an active choice, not a passive glance. When grief felt all-consuming, I would deliberately turn my thoughts to what was unseen. I would think about my son in heaven, God's eternal purpose, and the promise of reunion. I would picture him in the arms of Jesus, and I still do this today, years later.

The things we can see in our physical world are all temporary. The pregnancy tests that will never show positive again, the ultrasound photos we'll never get to take, the tiny footprints that mark both hello and goodbye—these are temporary. They're painfully real to us at the moment. But they're not the end of the story.

What's eternal is the love we carry for our babies. It's the hope we have in Christ and the promise of a future reunion in heaven. When we fix our eyes on those things, those beautiful things, we can start to move forward in a different light.

I remember sitting in our little house, snow on the ground outside. The visible signs of loss surrounded me. Little mementos from Bodhi's birth sat in one box. Sympathy ornaments hung on the Christmas tree. Worship music was on in the background. And the trees outside were bare, just like I felt.

At the time, I was choosing to focus on what I could physically see. I was choosing to focus on the devastation of the loss because that's exactly what you do when you lose someone. It is all-consuming, and that is normal.

To really move through grief and eventually pick it up and purposefully take it along with you, you have to fully feel it first.[IP] You have to sob at inopportune times, get angry with God, question why your life has been ruined, feel guilty, and really sit in the sorrow.

The pain is there for a purpose, and while Jesus didn't cause it, He will get you through it. He will be the light of a perfect verse when you need it, the worship song that brings the tears, and the most incredible listener you could imagine.

I sat in my own sorrow for a very long time before I realized that I couldn't take this on by myself. I needed to turn to God. I needed to trust that He would help me move forward.

So, instead, I started focusing on what I couldn't physically see. I couldn't see my son, but I could trust he was being held in heaven. I couldn't see God's purpose, but I could trust that He had a good one. I couldn't see the future, but I could trust it was held in hands far more capable than my own.

Don't misunderstand me here. I'm not telling you to ignore your present grief or pretend it doesn't hurt. No, you *must* walk through that dark, heavy, terrible valley to see the beauty on the other side.

In this verse, Paul wasn't suggesting we deny our earthly struggles. Rather, he was offering us a perspective that could sustain us through them. When we fix our eyes on the eternal, it doesn't remove our pain, but it does give us hope beyond it.[IP]

The temporary nature of our time on Earth doesn't diminish the significance of our losses. Instead, it reminds us that our story doesn't end here. Every tear, every ache, every moment of grief is seen and known by a God who promises that one day, all things will be made new.

As we get close to the end of this journey together, I want to remind you that grief will always be part of your story. There will still be moments when the weight of loss feels heavy. There will be holidays and birthdays and due dates that come along and blindside you with pain you thought you had already dealt with.

There will be times when you want to toss your pack of grief into the abyss and run. But that's just grief. That's the nature of this difficult, terrible path we're on.

But we can choose, again and again, to fix our eyes on what is unseen and eternal. We can hold onto the promise that one day, we will see clearly what we now only see through eyes of faith.

Our babies are not only memories, but they are living souls in the presence of God. The love we have for them isn't a remnant of what was but a preview of what will be.

While we remain here, carrying our grief, they dwell in the eternal reality we can only glimpse through faith. With faith, we can imagine that when we get to heaven one day, we'll hear a tiny voice say, "Hi, Mama." Can you imagine? Sometimes, this glimpse of faith is the only thing that can get me through the day.

So when grief feels overwhelming, when the visible signs of loss threaten to consume you, remember to fix your eyes on what is unseen. Remember that your baby is more alive than ever in the presence of God. Remember that your tears are temporary, but your hope is eternal.

While grief may be our constant companion, it is not our final destination. What we see now is temporary, but what awaits us—and what our babies already experience—is gloriously, beautifully eternal.

Stepping Stones

Picture Heaven

- I want you to imagine your baby in heaven. What do they look like? Who are they with? What are they doing? What's the environment like around them? If you've accepted Jesus into your life and believe in Him, you will be saved and will be able to greet your baby in heaven one day. Picture it exactly how you see it, and have faith that it will happen.

Conclusion

As you've moved through the sections of this book, we've discussed how grief is a journey. Grief will never fully leave you, and you will always think about your baby because you will always love them deeply. I can promise that it will not always be as painful as the first few months if you do the work to process your grief. Pain and joy can coexist, and I hope my life is a testimony to that.

When we first enter the valley of grief after losing a baby, the darkness feels impenetrable. In those early days, when the pain is raw and the tears flow freely, it's impossible to imagine ever finding purpose in such profound loss. These feelings of pain, anger, guilt, and questioning are normal, and they reflect the depth of our love for our precious babies.

Yet, as we begin to walk through the valley, we discover we're not alone on this path. God walks beside us, even when we can't feel His presence. Sometimes we wonder if He's even hearing us. Keep moving forward, one step at a time. Keep doing the work to become a better version of you each day, closer to the image that God has for you.

Gradually, you'll begin to see a little bit of light. While many of us wish our grief would disappear, it doesn't. But

The Valley Between

because our eyes adjust to seeing hope even in darkness, we eventually learn that joy and sorrow can coexist. We can miss our babies fiercely while still embracing the life we were meant to live.

In discovering God's strength, we find we can carry what once felt unbearable. When our own strength isn't enough, His sustains us. When our faith wavers, His remains steady. We learn to lean into His strength instead of depleting our own. We rely on Him more than we do ourselves. We begin to surrender.

Finally, we discover that our journey through grief might actually have meaning behind it. There might be a purpose we never could have believed would be there. Some of us find ourselves supporting other grieving parents. Others create ministries or support groups. And others quietly share their story with someone who needs to hear they're not alone.

This doesn't mean our grief ends when we begin to see a greater purpose. It doesn't. We will always miss our babies, always wonder about the milestones we didn't get to celebrate, always feel that empty space in our hearts that belongs only to them. But we learn to carry our grief differently. It becomes part of our story, and not our whole story.[IP]

As you close this book, remember that wherever you are in your journey, whether still in the depths of grief or beginning to see purpose through your pain, your path is your own. There's no timeline for healing, no "right way" to grieve. Your baby matters. Your story matters. Your grief matters. Take all the time you need to process your loss and give space for what's next.

This valley of grief will change you forever. But we carry with us the promise that one day, every tear will be wiped away, every broken heart will be healed, and every question will be answered. Until then, we walk forward in hope, carrying our babies in our hearts and trusting that even this deep valley is not without purpose.

Acknowledgments

This book would not exist without my husband, Travis. Thank you for your unwavering encouragement and for gently pushing me forward when I doubted myself. Your belief in this project and in me has been my anchor throughout this journey. I am forever grateful for your support, patience, and love.

To all the brave mothers who have trusted me with their stories of loss and grief—your vulnerability and courage have left me humbled and inspired. Thank you for opening your hearts, for sharing your babies with me, and for allowing me to witness both your pain and your strength. Your experiences have shaped this book in ways I could never have imagined, and I hope these pages honor the sacred journey we share.

And to Bodhi—I'm so thankful God chose me to be your mama. Your brief life forever changed mine, and this book is one of the many ways your legacy continues to touch hearts.

About the Author

Dr. Jenna Zigler is an optometrist turned entrepreneur. After her company, Eye Love, was acquired in 2021, she shifted her focus to something even closer to her heart: giving back. She now serves as Vice President of the Eye Believe Foundation, an organization born out of her and her husband's deep passion for providing the gift of sight to underserved communities.

In addition to her work in eye care, she's embarking on a new project centered on grief—a deeply personal journey. After her experience with the loss of her son, she felt a calling to help others navigate the often overwhelming landscape of grief. Her project aims to help those walking through this type of grief find hope in their heartache, strength in their story, and purpose in their pain so that they can be fully present in this life they were given.

Previously, Jenna owned and operated two optometry practices along with her husband, which were sold in 2017 to focus on Eye Love and other projects. Outside of work, she enjoys running, traveling the world, exploring new restaurants, and playing with her two young sons.

Connect with Jenna at JennaZigler.com

LISTEN TO
THE VALLEY BETWEEN
ON AUDIBLE TODAY

As someone who has walked this path, I know how overwhelming grief can feel.

Join our community waitlist today, and you'll get weekly messages of hope and encouragement delivered straight to your inbox.

The community offers:

- Weekly, faith-based video support calls
- Guest appearances from therapists, coaches, and mental health professionals
- Completely private and secure space - no social media, no public access

CONNECT WITH JENNA

Follow Her on Facebook or Visit JennaZigler.com Today.

 @DrJennaZigler

JennaZigler.com

Miscarriage and Pregnancy Loss Support Group

FIND SUPPORT IN THIS FREE FACEBOOK GROUP FOR WOMEN WHO HAVE LOST A BABY.

THIS BOOK IS PROTECTED INTELLECTUAL PROPERTY

The author of this book values Intellectual Property and has utilized Instant IP, a groundbreaking technology. Instant IP is the patented, blockchain-based solution for Intellectual Property protection.

Blockchain is a distributed public digital record that can not be edited. Instant IP timestamps the author's ideas, creating a smart contract, thus an immutable digital asset that proves ownership and establishes a first to use / first to file event.

Protected by Instant IP ™

LEARN MORE AT INSTANTIP.TODAY

www.ingramcontent.com/pod-product-compliance
Lightning Source LLC
Chambersburg PA
CBHW052147070526
44585CB00017B/2008